Diet and Exercise Impact Cholesterol

Amit S

Abstract

Cholesterol, a crucial lipid molecule, plays a pivotal role in various physiological functions, yet its imbalance can lead to detrimental health outcomes, particularly cardiovascular diseases. This paper provides a thorough examination of the intricate relationship between diet, exercise, and cholesterol levels, encompassing a wide range of studies and research findings. With a focus on both dietary patterns and physical activity, we delve into the multifaceted mechanisms through which these lifestyle factors influence cholesterol metabolism and, consequently, overall cardiovascular health.

The first section elucidates the significance of cholesterol, distinguishing between low-density lipoprotein cholesterol (LDL-C) and high-density lipoprotein cholesterol (HDL-C). While LDL-C is often termed "bad cholesterol" due to its association with atherosclerosis, HDL-C is recognized as "good cholesterol," exerting protective effects on the cardiovascular system.

The subsequent sections explore the impact of diet on cholesterol levels. Various dietary patterns, such as the Mediterranean diet, DASH (Dietary Approaches to Stop Hypertension) diet, and low-fat diets, are scrutinized in terms of their efficacy in modulating cholesterol profiles. Nutritional components, including saturated fats, trans fats, dietary fibers, and omega-3 fatty acids, are dissected to unveil their differential effects on cholesterol metabolism. Additionally, the role of dietary cholesterol itself is explored, challenging previous assumptions about its direct correlation with blood cholesterol levels.

Moving on, the paper delves into the intricate relationship between exercise and cholesterol regulation. Regular physical activity has been consistently associated with favorable changes in cholesterol levels, notably an increase in HDL-C and a decrease in LDL-C. The mechanisms behind these effects involve enhanced enzymatic activity, improved lipoprotein particle size, and increased expression of genes related to lipid metabolism. Different forms of exercise, including aerobic and resistance training, are evaluated to discern their specific impacts on cholesterol metabolism.

An integral aspect of the analysis is the interplay between diet and exercise. Studies examining the combined effects of a healthy diet and regular physical activity reveal synergistic benefits in optimizing cholesterol profiles. The intricate signaling pathways that mediate these synergies are explored, shedding light on the potential for personalized lifestyle interventions tailored to an individual's metabolic needs.

The paper also addresses the role of genetics in mediating the response to diet and exercise interventions. Genetic factors influence an individual's predisposition to hypercholesterolemia and their response to dietary and exercise interventions. Understanding the interplay between genetic factors and lifestyle modifications is crucial for developing personalized approaches to cholesterol management.

In conclusion, this comprehensive analysis highlights the nuanced relationship between diet, exercise, and cholesterol levels. A holistic understanding of these interactions is essential for developing effective preventive and therapeutic strategies for cardiovascular diseases. As we navigate the complex landscape of cholesterol management, the integration of personalized approaches that consider individual variations in genetics, lifestyle, and metabolic response will be paramount in promoting cardiovascular health.

TABLE OF CONTENTS

LIST OF TABLES

CHAPTER I

INTRODUCTION

The modern world that we are living in today is built by social animals, i.e., we the HUMANS or traditionally, it's the MAN. This modern world is built up on various criteria and amongst which, the vital focus is on evolution. When the word evolution is referred, it is actually the emphasis on the CHANGE that results in an evolution. While we try to connect the evolution with the structure and physique of a human, it all started with the physical activities that a man did, to survive in the early ages. These physical activities included hunting, food gathering to survive in contingencies, fishing for food, moving from one place to another that included swimming, walking, running etc to wander around either to attack or to rescue from enemies, etc. The physical activities that the man performed helped him to achieve the three basic necessities that is, food, clothing and shelter. On achieving these, Man gathered knowledge of the usage of natural resources for his survival such as agriculture, storage of water from rivers and ponds, etc, which introduced various other forms of physical activities and built up his strength, resistance, power and developed his overall personality.

While in the 21st century, survival has its own different meaning. It is said that, if education is one side of the coin then the other is physical fitness. and this is a outcome of an properly balanced development of mind and body. This balance is achieved with education that maximizes the mental ability and the education of the physique that maximizes the endurance of the body to work under any circumstances that include stress, climatic changes, work pressure, etc. Moreover, if education teaches of how to do certain things, then physical education teaches about the will power and endurance to attain the preset goals and aims.

In the present scenario, where the human life has attainted enormous knowledge on each and every field, the physical education too has its own importance in each and everyone's lives. Sports are like nervous system for attainment of one's overall personality development, as they help a man stay physically fit. To even talk nationally, the countries that are focusing on sports are far developed than those countries that don't. Sports have become the favorite spice of every individual's life.

Sports may be played with an intention to strengthen the muscles or for leisure; the ultimate result is physical fitness and thus, with the passage of time, man has realized the importance of physical activities and sports of various forms, to attain a physically fit body. To talk about sports the other way round, it is a means of having fun, experiencing thrill, etc and also inculcating the qualities of strategy building, courage, patience and having the zeal.

The greatest Buzz words of today's world revolve a lot around sports, exercises, physical culture, gymnastics, fitness, etc. These are all competitive in nature but at the same time it pulls down the concentration as a whole on the overall development of personality and overall fitness which is certainly not possible without sports. This is so, because the modern world is extremely competitive and one cannot succeed with mere mental ability and zero physical fitness. This happens because may it be any field, a wholesome personality is preferred that is good at both, ideological reasoning with required educational and mental abilities i.e. qualification in brief; as well as sustaining the workload at any circumstance with durability and resistance that requires one to be physically fit.

History of Bodybuilding:

The muscle building is a physical culture that has attracted a huge number of followers since ages together, even before the word bodybuilding or competition came into existence. But, when it comes to the history of bodybuilding the major recognition came from the society of Greek and Egypt. In the former stage the activity of weight training was considered as an athletic activity in general, performed with an aim for strength gaining purpose as well as for the measurement of power in the ancient Greek and Egyptian society. They considered the weight training exercises as a means of transforming a powerless body into a powerful one with endurance. In order to train one self, stone of different weights and a number of sizes were primarily used for the purpose of strength training. The development of muscle achieved through the process of weight training and strength training, was considered as one of the celebration of the great human body, which was one of the innovative idea of the Greeks.

Physical culture and bodybuilding may same to be similar, but are different from each other. But on the contrary they have close relationship with each other. Physical culture referrers to the habit of exercising, either out of necessity (hunting, fishing, horse riding, swimming cross ponds or lakes or rivers, etc) or because of hobbit (running, walking, playing outdoor and indoor games etc). The main aim of physical culture is to achieve over all physical fitness, which is as referred above, due to necessities or hobbits. Whereas, bodybuilding is a sport, that beholds a precise idea within itself. Bodybuilding is considered as a skill and activity that is performed with an aim to achieve the development of muscles. The major intention behind bodybuilding is to acquire enormous power, strength, physical endurance and more over achieving a visibility a well built and beautifully transformed muscular body. Initially, in order to acquire the enhancement of stamina, longitivity and overall health nals were made use of (the stone dumbbells weights of various sizes are known as nals).

It was in the early 1890s, Mr. Eugene Sandow, the one on whom the statuette of Mr. Olympic is modeled, took the bodybuilding skill to a different level. It is well known to all the followers that the process of bodybuilding exercises got a kick start since the introduction of iron game.

All about Mr. Eugene Sandow,

The bodybuilding activity which is all about the art of demonstration of well built muscles actually didn't exist even in the beginning of 19th century. It was in the late 19th century, a man named Eugene Sandow, who belongs to Prussia, promoted it and gave it immense important which has lasted even today. For his initiation and contribution towards bodybuilding, is known as "The Father of Modern Bodybuilding".

He is the one who holds the credit of begin an establisher of the bodybuilding sports, as he was the one who provided the enjoyment of the view of his well built physique to the audience. He enjoyed his performance of muscle display and astonished the audiences and gave them a thrilling experience of watching him flexing, demonstrating strength, wrestling, etc. he was a man who believed in innovation and invention in his later life he turned into an entrepreneur by creating a large number of business around his farm.

He was the first person who marketed his products that were branded with his own name. Further, when he gained popularity, he holds the complete credit of invention of selling various exercises equipments for the first time ever. The equipments of exercises that he sold on mass basis included tension bands, dumbbells, machined dumbbells, spring pulley, etc.

With the invention of new reforms in bodybuilding brought forward by Mr. Eugene Sandow, had brought about a huge revolution, in the field of physical culture. By the end of 19th century, a birth of new system of training had taken place and weight training had a different view and meaning for many. The ancient and traditional stone lifting process to built body had now turned into a proficient practice of weight training. Now on, the weight lifting or strength training not only served the propose of entertainment but also served to be a source of achieving overall physical fitness that accompanied power, endurance, highly developed stamina, through these advance physical culture.

It could be seen and evaluated by every spectator and audiences that weight lifting and it effects were not a natural evolution but a innovated primitive practice of lifting stones that later emerged into advance strength training practice with weights and dumbbells. The actual intention of bodybuilding was not only to develop a wonderful physique but also to amaze the crowds with immense strength and display of power. Ultimately the outcome was the gain of intense favoritism and interest among the people for weight training.

The major popularity for bodybuilding and weight training was gained between the time periods of early 1890 to 1929. It was not only a challenging phase for the strong men who accepted the skill of bodybuilding and implemented it with great efforts, continuous practice and hard work. More over as the time past and rigorous practices were done to build body, an unexpected power strengthening was witnessed among the men who were involved in weight training. Later these men could easily involve themselves in pulling carts, lifting various animals differing in size and weights etc. This view was a source of amusement, excitement, thrill and enjoyment for the public.

The "Golden Age"

From the traditional time to the time phase that we witness today, the period from 1940 to 1970 is known as the "Golden Age" of bodybuilding keeping into consideration all the evolution that took place in the field of bodybuilding. Especially at the time of world war II there was self realization on the part of men worldwide with regards to bodybuilding had taken place. These men had now realized that physical strength and a bigger, stronger and aggressive personality could add up to the strength of their nation. Hence, after that bodybuilding got immense acceptance and popularity worldwide. The men were now aware of the fact that to win over various challenges of life, it was very important to be a source of strength and good physique. And accordingly the love and attraction towards bodybuilding grew on a continuous basis.

The well known bodybuilders of this age were Clancy Ross, Steve Reeves, Larry Scott, Bill Pearl and Reg Park. Further in the year 1939, the AAU, i.e., the Amateur Athletic Union added a competition in the existing bodybuilding and weight lifting contest which had later got popularized as AAU Mr. America. But in the succeeding year 1940, a large number of bodybuilders were extremely disappointed as this competition was conducted only for the amateur bodybuilders and its major focus was on promoting the weight lifting sport at the Olympics.

To overcome the issues that are being stated, two brothers named Ben Weider and Joe Weider came together and formed IFBB i.e. the International Federation of Body Builders and then started conducting body building competitions under the same organization and named it as IFBB Mr. America. Now, this competition was kept open for all the professional athletes as well. With this the AAU lost its importance and the IFBB gained its popularity among the people.

Later in the year 1950, one more organization was formed which was NABBA i.e. National Amateur Body Builders Association, which conducted Bodybuilding and Weightlifting Competitions in UK and named it as NABBA Mr. Universe. And the latest of all is the Mr. OLYMPIA which was first conducted in the year 1965 and is famous till today and it is considered as one of the glorious and prestigious title of bodybuilding that any bodybuilder could possess till date.

The living legend of Bodybuilding- Arnold Schwarzenegger (since 1970s)

The field of bodybuilding and its craze had reached its highest peak in the 1970s and the whole credit goes to Mr. Arnold Schwarzenegger. He is the living icon of bodybuilding who has given tremendous contribution towards the field of bodybuilding throughout his life time. Pumping Iron, a film released in the year 1977, in which Mr. Arnold Schwarzenegger played the lead and astonished the audience with his marvelous physique and huge musculature. Due to the promotion made by him for bodybuilding, compared to any other fitness sports, bodybuilding started gaining a large number of popularity in the whole world.

Arnold started lifting weight when he was just fifteen years old. Some of his first achievement was the Junior Mr. Europe contest in the year 1965. When he won Mr. Universe he was only twenty years old. Further he has won Mr. Olympia seven times in his life time. He has also contributed towards bodybuilding by writing various books and a number of articles on the bodybuilding sports. The well known Arnold Sports Festival is known to be the second most popular and vital bodybuilding event on professional basis. He was nick named as the Austrian Oak due to his long lasting and endured physical fitness. He was also the 38th Governor of California (2003-2011).

It was in the 1990s when Mr. Arnold Schwarzenegger became the chairman of the President Council of Fitness and inspired a large public of America to become fit and active in their lives. He did this by doing various practices and activity related to bodybuilding. May it be conducting bodybuilding events or he himself getting down on the streets to interact with people and pose for them, he made use of every opportunity that he could explore to promote fitness and bodybuilding. Even today at the age of 71, he works out and motivates the youth by organizing various fitness programs, seminars, rally, weightlifting competition and Arnold Classic bodybuilding competitions.

Reference: Arnold Schwarzenegger (1985), "Encyclopedia of Modern Bodybuilding", Simon & Schuster, New York,

Bodybuilding in India:

In India gym tradition got popular after 16th century onwards. But weight training was not considered to be professional and only few those who were interested could approach gym for weight training.

It took a great struggle during 16th century to make gym tradition famous in India. As wrestling in Akhada or Taleem were very popular and at every corner of streets in India and introducing weight training was a difficult task. But as days passed, people started getting aware of the new sports bodybuilding because of world popularity of Arnold Schwarzenegger and other leading bodybuilders. Gym tradition gained momentum in India. Everyone defined bodybuilding as the training and diet to develop body specially muscles for exhibitive purpose as we know it today.

If we noticed Indian history, we observed that every year our interest in physical culture has grown throughout the various ages. In 1100s there are evidence of details descriptions of diet, training and lifestyles of famous sportsman's. During that time free squats and pushups were common daily exercises and weight training was done by using stones and sacks of sands. By 1500s bodybuilding has gain popularity and youths were passionate about it. That time, Nals were used as weights for dumbbells and plates which were made from stones with a hoop in centre and a wooden thick stick were inserted in between the stone making it as a handle of dumbbell or bar.

When British invaded India, least importance was given to physical education and health issue, amongst the country people. In 1905, the interest was regenerated, mainly in strand pulling. This was due to a great popularity of Sandow visit to India in 1904.

In 1920s, a Burmese man by name Chit Tun, who was settled in Calcutta, made the muscle control game of bodybuilding introduced in India. Even though visit of Sandow and bodybuilders of other countries made their shown in our country the craze for bodybuilding was not up to the mark. In 1930 Prof. K.V.Iyer was the most famous instructor of that time. Mr. Iyer set up Hercules Gym in Bangalore and started first postal course in muscle display.

B.C.Ghosh credits Chit Tun for motivating him to train in muscle display. In 1930 Mr.Gosh and his co-partner Mr.K.C.Sen Gupta installed a gym in Calcutta. Ghosh and Sengupta were the initial trained both Monotosh Roy and Monahar Aich and later they become classic bodybuilders of 50th era.

History of Belagavi Body Building:

Since 1955 Bodybuilders of Belagavi district bodybuilders are participating in various National Bodybuilding Competitions. Now at present, Bodybuilding sports is very popular in Belagavi district. Mr. Katti first started taking bodybuilding competitions restricted for gym. As per the knowledge of the senior most bodybuilder, Mr. L.R.Patil, the history of bodybuilding began from Samarth Gymnasium the oldest gym of Belagavi.

In 1998, B.D.B.B.A (Belagavi District Bodybuilding Association) was formed under the noble guidance of Mr. Sunil Aptekar (National Judge), Prakash Pujari (National Judge), who were the founder members of association. Mr Ajit Siddnavar, Bandu Majurkar, L R Patil were the association. This association is responsible to conduct Mr. Belagavi District Competition and send Belagavi team to state and national competitions.

These competitions were very famous for the bodybuilders like Premchand Degara (Mr. Universe), Prasad Kumar of Service, Sunil Aptekar of Railways etc, who used to come from outside as a guest poser and seeing their Hercules physique and ability of displaying muscles, Belagavi people used to get amazed and their curiosity and love for bodybuilding started increasing.

In 1998, BDBBA (Belgaum District Bodybuilders Association) got well established under noble guidance of Shri Sunil N Aptekar (National Judge and Inter-National Bodybuilder), Prakash Pujari (National Judge) who were the founder members of the association. Mr. Ajit Siddnavar, Bandu Majukar, L.R.Patil were in the association. This association was responsible to conduct Mr. Belagum District Competition and send Belgaum team to State and National competitions.

In the year 2003, BDBBA conducted Sr. National (Mr. India) competition at the Belgaum and several bodybuilders from Belgaum participated and secured prizes and brought fame to the city.

Shri L.R.Patil is now no more but Maratha Yuvak Sangh members still conduct the Belgaum Shree competition in the memory of Late Shri L.R.Patil. Since 54 years they receive sponsorship from Roasaheb Gogte (Industrialist), Polyhydron Company, etc, to conduct the competition. But the main preference for making bodybuilding popular in Belagavi, conducting Belgaum Shree competition for motivating people of city and making awareness of Bodybuilding sports goes to Maratha Yuvak Sangh,

Why Belagavi District is Famous for Bodybuilding?

Bodybuilding purely depends upon muscular endurance. Muscular endurance can be defined as, "It is the ability of muscle to do the activity for longer time without getting fatigue". There are so many reasons why Belagavi district is famous in bodybuilding.

There are so many bodybuilders in Belagavi district who have won National and International Championships. The bodybuilders belonging to the city usually work hard for their daily bread, so it is bit natural that they will be strong and determined towards their aim. Most of the bodybuilders are from remote paces and are not financial fit, many of bodybuilders have an ambition to achieve place in National competitions so that they could get job through sports quota. But till they get job, bodybuilders of this city do jobs like cable work, delivering milk, peon in reputed institution, coach and gym instructors. No matter how they hard have to work whole day they never give up their routine of gym exercises. Due to this they have developed strong zeal in them to become a good bodybuilder.

The other reason for bodybuilding to be popular is the active Bodybuilders Association. They conduct competitions regularly and given rewards and cash prizes to all winners. Such promotion and encourages leading bodybuilders to perform at their peak.

These are few prominent bodybuilders of Belagavi

Shri Sunil.N.Aptekar, Shri Ranjit.K.Killekar, Anil Killekar, Nitin Jadhav, Raju Bhatkhande, Sandeep Bhatkande, Vishal Teware, Ranjit Jadhav, Noor Sanadi, Sandeep Patil, Vikas Shahapurkar and many more.

Physical Fitness:

As said by a great Philosopher a healthy mind resides in a healthy body it means mentality ability and excellence in anybody's life greatly depends on the level on fitness achieved by one self. The field of sports and the world of games are such that a lot of factor influence it. One of the major factors that intensely influence the success in sports is the physical fitness. It can be rather consider that one of the key to lead a balanced life is to stay physically fitness. The other factors that influence physical fitness are the physical wellbeing, emotional status, social status, spiritual appeal, over all views and expression towards life etc.

Moreover, to be precise, the logic behind why an individual is bound to be responsible to maintain his/her physical fitness is very simple. If an individual is not physical fit it depicts that the life that is been lead is very clumsy and lazy. Due to this it results in a condition where the body starts ruling the mind and which is not all a positive sign. On the contrary, if an individual is physically fit, it shows that his or her mind is controlling the body effectively and the overall way of living of the individual is healthy and active.

Fitness of the physique is the mark of victory in the life of human beings because that not only inculcates a healthy lifestyle but also brings about a harmonious balance in the mind and body. And when this is achieved, getting hold of anything else in life seems extremely easier. As the physical fitness is not about excelling but it is actually about increasing the capacity and chances of achieving excellence. (According to Johnson and Nelson, 1982)

To be more focused, the field of body building too has its own importance for the achievement of physical fitness. Because it is obvious that to achieve a good physique and an excellent musculature, if there is something that supports the diet plans, hard work put in for weight training, determination, dedication and zeal, then that is the physical fitness. To perform highly intense workout plans of weight training, the physical fitness of a bodybuilder plays an important role. When it is the matter of building muscles, the most important factor to have effect on an individual, is his level of capacity and efficiency to perform workouts and keep going throughout the workout session even after reaching a phase where an individual feels extremely fatigued and impossible to keep going.

The biological efficiency that is executed by a bodybuilder to train himself through weights, is achieved through a motor skills and performing capacity with total fitness. Thus in a field like sports, greater achievements are achieved with physical fitness and skill training. And physical fitness alone is never built up in a day. It is a result of continuous efforts and maintenance of consistency in building the fitness of an individual's body. Overall impression of physical fitness is mainly about the stamina development that is required for performing various forms of exercises.

The Bodybuilding Physique:

Creation of just muscle mass does not lead an individual to become a good and efficient bodybuilder. Rather each and every part of the body has to be trained in all possible angles to that an appropriate size and shape of the muscles is achieved. This is to be done to stimulate all the muscles of the body and all the fibers that are involved in it. This stimulation is only possible when the muscles are trained in a manner that they acquire the desired shape and required mass with the length of time acquainted to achieve the same.

This is what makes a bodybuilder look different from other sport persons such as the swimmers, weight lifters, footballers, athletes, etc. So the body and muscle transformation that is required to achieve, can only be possible with overall balanced and shaped musculature. Thus to attain such developed body, one needs to know the correct technique of doing the same. The changes that a bodybuilders body goes through such as the peak of the arms, huge and well shaped upper and lower body, peaky calf muscles, pectoral and deltoid muscle, broad and defined chest, etc, are never occurred as a sudden unexpected result of just exercise, but rather it is a result of correct technique that the bodybuilder has used to exercise himself with respective weights leads to such changes that are expected as end result.

Therefore according to the Encyclopedia of Bodybuilding, by Mr. Arnold (1985), the most excellent bodybuilder is the one who knows the right technique and the various things that the right techniques include are the knowledge about how the tissue in a muscle actually works, which exercise can affect the muscle in what manner, how to achieve the expected results in the body through training, different techniques needed for transforming the muscles from lean to huge and full of mass yet with minimal fat, etc.

Sports and Bodybuilding:

It is not long ago that the coaches of various sports kept their trainees far away from the bodybuilding through weight training. The reason behind this is that, traditionally the sport of bodybuilding is considered was believed to make the muscles rigid which further leads to loss of flexibility in the trainees. But in the real scenario, this is turned out to be only a myth because bodybuilding and weight training not only builds muscles, but also builds strength, power, durability, resistance, endurance, stamina and also makes an individual capable of handling any level of hardcore training required for sports for that matter.

Now, if the present scenario of sports training is observed, there is not a single sport where the bodybuilding and weight training methods are not implemented to train the sports trainees. To be precise, the actual bodybuilding training is given to these sports persons while training them in their respective sports.

One of the successful high jumpers over the period of time Mr. Dwight stones, gave a maximum number of days of each week to train himself with weights. He did so because he encountered diminishing returns with the regular type of training that he was undergoing since a number of succeeding years of sports training. Later he was not able to cope up for further excellence and finally ended up weight training his good self and rose in the field of High Jump sports all over again. This so happened because with the help of weight training, he gained excellent control on the neuromuscular coordination which is a must to become a successful sportsman.

Sports persons like Stones are those who require a training which could help them in building strength increasing consistency, overall conditioning of the body, etc. this is a combination of requirement of the body of such sportspersons which cannot be attained without weight training. So this is the best of best an athlete or a sportsperson can do for himself by including the weight training program in his schedule along with other sports trainings. The only key to success in the field of sports is a good neuromuscular coordination which is well acquired with weight training for achievement of athletic performance at a greater level of significance.

For instance, swimmers are known for their endurance and resistance in the limbs that is acquired by swimming in water on a regular basis. But this does not help the swimmers to increase the strength in the muscles as due to rigorously working on the limbs there is every possible chance that they start facing diminishing returns.

Bodybuilding and flexibility:

Bodybuilding and weight training are those aspects that have gained immense popularity in today's world and are like a must in the world that we live in today. But the acceptance and liking among people for the sport has taken some time because this was something that could simply transform the whole outlook of the body. so to let this happen people had to undergo a number of changes such as being mentally prepared, move beyond the feelings of worry, etc.

Muscle Bound is a phenomenon that states a condition where in a body will lose its flexibility to perform any kind of activity. Traditionally, it was considered that the condition called muscle bound used to arise with the practice of weight training and bodybuilding. It was very common to go through such feelings because a bodybuilder's body looked extremely rigid and hardcore like any rock. So various hypotheses were built up regarding the same and one among them was about the condition called Muscle Bound.

To speak about on the contrary, in the real sense it is not at all true. This is so because the practice of Bodybuilding and weight training actually brings about a wholesome development in the fibers of the muscle. It not only trains the fibers but also increases or enhances the growth of the muscle fibers. Due to this not only the strength of the muscle is gained but also the power and flexibility of the muscles is increased to a greater level. And when this happens, there is every possibility that an exclusive endurance is built up in the muscle to resist and sustain any kind of physical activity there on.

The logic to be applied here is very simple. It's the rule of contradictory nature of muscle. This means that in the practice of weight training, when one muscle is contracted the opposite muscle will be stretched. When this happens regularly the flexibility of the muscle is rather improved than to decline. However to enhance the level of flexibility, the modern bodybuilders adopt a routine of stretching workouts and yoga, before and after the weight training exercises.

Enhancing Aerobic Endurance with Bodybuilding:

When the word endurance is to be explained in terms of Bodybuilding and weight training, it can be differentiated with two different aspects, i.e. cardiovascular endurance and muscular endurance. These two are significantly different from each other but are still interrelated. The term muscular endurance means that to ensure maximum repetitions of any set of exercise, it is very important to engage a huge number of muscle fibers while performing the exercise.

In human body, we find huge muscles in the lower part of body, it is our thigh muscles. In our daily routine we use our thigh muscle for every type of work, for every moment we take help of our thigh muscles. We can say, unintentionally we will be giving much workout to thigh muscles. In a day, we couldn't imagine how many steps we climb, how many steps we walk or run, how much we stretch our quadriceps and hamstring muscles or how many times we have done sit ups. These all exercises we perform unintentionally without imagining how much training load we are giving to our thigh muscles without doing workout.

Therefore training legs muscles is the most challenging part for bodybuilders. Because while training leg muscles when you are doing heavy squatting you will get tired quickly this happens because leg muscles fibers will be accumulated with lactic acid formation resulting into fatigue of muscle fibers before you go through all the sets of workout. If one wants to do complete workout routine then they should know how to add fibers.

Whereas, the cardio vascular stamina involves the performing capability of heart, lungs as well as circulatory system of the body and ensures sufficient blood supply to one's body while performing any set of exercises. The best example which will be suitable for the above mentioned statement is running, after a long interval from exercises suddenly if you performed running for a long distance your legs will get tired soon and you will end up breathing heavy. This will not happen because of muscle fibers of legs. But the failure caused due to the insufficient oxygen supply to muscles to get rid of lactic acid formed in muscles.

Bodybuilding' training is to increase the volume of efforts to achieve the desirable effect. This will lead to increase in the muscular endurance. But even bodybuilders do posses cardiovascular endurance as they workout with a comfort zone to avoid cardiovascular failure. This doesn't mean bodybuilders are good runners. With that massive body weight if they want to be a good runner then they have to train hard to carry body weight and run.

Cardio vascular endurance is very essential for bodybuilder muscular endurance. Because of hard training lactic acid formation will be developed in muscles. If heart, lungs and circulation system produces enough oxygen during the workout for the specific working muscle, the lactic acid is processed once again in the body to create energy. This prevents the muscle from muscle failure that occurs because of later contraction.

This is the reason why a lot of body builders are developing their aerobic system by doing different cardiovascular training like, running, swimming, cycling etc.

Bodybuilding with relation to Fitness:

Bodybuilding and weight training are one of those sports that build up enormous fitness levels in the human body. The only way through which the fitness is built up is by strengthening the muscles by making them work efficiently within a given time frame, by development of tone, increased level of blood flow and enhancing better supply of oxygen towards the muscles so as to make them work with efficiency during the workouts sessions.

After all it all matters with regards to how you train the muscle. If controlled amount of weights are included with increased number of sets, one can also get rid of the lower back pain that is usually encountered by the bodybuilders. And this is the major difference between power lifters and bodybuilders. While the power lifters are bound to push themselves with larger amount of weights, the bodybuilders can still build themselves with the controlled amount of weights with various levels of resistance that could be involved in the same.

All that is focally required is the technique of training the bodybuilders that is extremely important in terms of fitness. Only the technique needs to be taken care of and there will not be a single chance of injury in the bodybuilding sport. Besides there are normal consequences like any other sport for the bodybuilding sport too, such as the muscle soreness, temporary fatigue, minor sprain on occasional basis, temporary strains, etc.

Importance of Tanning in Bodybuilding:

Tanning is a process that enables a body to produce new melanin. Muscle building and muscle definition are two different aspects in the bodybuilding sport. When muscle building is concerned, it can be anyhow done with the help of an efficient trainer, who will train by keeping in mind all his prior experiences in the sport. But when it comes to muscle definition, it refers to the extra efforts that needs to be put in by the bodybuilders after the training sessions.

One of the most vital aspects of muscle definition is the technique of tanning the body. This helps in highlighting the muscles and the way they are built up.

Tan on body is achieved by exposing the skin to sun for at least half an hour to forty five minutes per day. Tan is that tool which provides a darker shade to the body and helps provide the developed muscles look well defined. Tanning also makes judgment easy for the judges to judge the bodybuilders during the competition. Tanning can be also done with the help of tanning parlors that make use of sunlamps to tan the body. Thus during the competitions conducted for bodybuilding, the light effects on the stage and tan on the body play a major role for judgments by mentors and flexing and execution of muscles by the bodybuilders.

Training and Bodybuilding:

To attain efficiency in any kind of sports, the skills required for the sports are extremely essential. Such skills are learnt through appropriate training methods which involve certain techniques which lead to enhancement of skills in the right way. The process of training involved in bodybuilding includes mainly the following factors like regularity, systematic movement towards the harder levels of weight training, progressive learning on the part of the bodybuilders, etc. during the process of training in bodybuilding, it is necessary to keep in mind the essentiality of balance between the mind and physic, to enhance the performance of the bodybuilders.

If the history is looked out, the gold medals are won by a series of small nations like the Korea, the Vietnam, the Japan, the Poland, etc for which only their efficient training techniques are responsible for their success. Such nations which may be tiny but the facilities and opportunities as well as the priority that the government gives is all that matters on a bigger note.

Many definitions are put forth by a number of philosophers and sportspersons which states the importance of training in bodybuilding and other sports discipline. As per these philosophers and sportspersons is not the infrastructure or the lavishing gym or ground that always matters but rather it is the coach, his experience and quality of teaching and training, how well he inculcates the culture of specific sports among the trainees, the delivery of mastery over the sport, etc is actually what really matters.

What does training meaningfully actually suggest?

To train meaningfully means to convert a common man into an extraordinary man with efficient training methods and techniques. It is all about bringing about a greater sense of efficiency, enhancement of performance and moreover benchmarking excellence among the trainees in the sport that is chosen by them. A human body can do wonders beyond imagination and only a coach or a trainer who is efficient enough can prove this.

An efficient trainer or a coach gives the trainees a set of qualities which are required to turn them into champions, some of them are zeal, determination, dedication, readiness to work had to any extent, extreme love for the sport chosen, priority for practice, consistency to achieve pre determined goals and above all, a trainer or a coach helps the trainees to set an aim for life with respect to the sports chosen by them.

What are lipoproteins?

Cholesterol is most excellent among all kinds of lipids. In other words it is partially both i.e. protein and lipid. Thus it is also known as lipoprotein.

Information of HDL and LDL:

Meaning and details of HDL cholesterol- HDL refers to High Density Lipoprotein Cholesterol, that glides through the blood stream. In this process, it eliminates bad cholesterol. Increased levels of HDL, prevents cardiac risk as well as related diseases and vice-versa. Daily continuous training, reduction of extra fat and avoiding smoking will raise the level of HDL levels.

The average man has an HDL cholesterol level of 30 to 75mg/dl. HDL levels of 60mg/dl or more then that provides security from cardiac diseases.

Meaning and details of LDL: LDL cholesterol refers to Low Density Lipoprotein, which is not considered to be good cholesterol. Increased levels of LDL are known to lead towards cardiac problem and vice versa. The average man has an LDL cholesterol level of 60 to 160 mg/dl. An LDL cholesterol level which is less than 100mg/dl is considered to be ideal.

Need of HDL and LDL in Bodybuilding:

It is a critical task when tries to improve the cholesterol profile. But when the cholesterol are kept under control it helps in enhancing once efforts of training and wholesome health. Different types of fruits are consumed by bodybuilders which includes more amounts of usually fats in the off season. This results in the risk of elevation of cholesterol to unexpected harmful levels. Thus balance levels of cholesterol are considered equal to overall good health.

The cholesterol called HDL ids considered to be Good Lipoprotein because it transports cholesterol away from the arterial walls. On the other hand LDL cholesterol is considered as Bad Lipoprotein because it takes alone cholesterol from the liver to the arteries where it deposits fatty like substance which is known as plaque in the arterial walls.

There are different types of necessity training patterns and diet plans. It has been listed that there are three forms of body i.e Ecto-morph, Meso-morph and Endo-morph that have their own unique characteristic.

Ectomorphs

Ectomorphs are extremely skinny and their main objective is to gain weight. They build will be light frame that have lean muscles and joints Ectomorphs exhibit elongated limbs and thin muscles and lack in strength and endurance. Their muscles development is very slow and requires putting on calories enough to ensure continued growth in their muscles.

Specification of Ectomorph:

- Thin skeleton composition
- Gaining weight is difficult
- Weak pectorals
- skinny shoulder but little wide
- good metabolism
- weight gain problem

Ectomorph body types find problems in gaining weight. They burn their calories very soon because of fast metabolism. They need to put on huge amount of calories to maintain weight gain.

The following tips for ectomorph body type will be beneficial:

- Include power training programs in their workout which could build more muscles mass and stay with basic exercises.
- Basic training workout will be beneficiary for them but with lots of rest in between the sets.
- Nutrition intake is very important; take more calories than your daily necessity and if required take weight gainer food supplements and protein too.
- Avoid running, swimming and any other vigorous activities to save burning of calories which are required to gain muscles and weight.

Mesomorph Body Types

Mesomorphs are naturally athletic physique, big muscles and large bone structure. They will find building of muscles very easy relatively to other body types. Mesomorph body type is ideal for development of muscles. But certainly have to include sufficient variety of workout pattern in their exercises routine to grow appropriate muscles and acquire a well built shape.

Specification of Mesomorph:

- Hard muscle
- Athletic
- Muscles defined
- Strong
- Easy muscle gain
- Gain weight more easily

Mesomorph gain quickly muscles or weight especially in the beginning stage. They respond well to weight training workout. The disadvantage of mesomorph is that they gain fat very soon and because of so, they need to watch on their calories input.

The following tips for mesomorph body type will be beneficial:

- Weight training and cardio workout will be useful for mesomorph body types. The more variety in their training program will surely bring muscle quality, symmetry and proportion.

- Long duration workout with minimum resting interval. Mesomorphic physique will respond well to such training programs.

- Plenty of protein with balanced diet and watching calorie intake will get transformed in an ideal physique.

Cholesterols

Cholesterols are important part of the brain's cell membrane, nerve cell and bile as well to aid the human body to soak up fat as well as fat-soluble vitamin. Our liver produces 80% cholesterols and the remaining is obtained by the body from foods like dairy products, fish, meat, eggs, etc. Vegan food does not consist of any kind of cholesterols. Cholesterols are used by human body to make vitamin D and various hormones such as estrogen, testosterone and cortisol.

Cholesterol is considered as lipids. A lipid is an organic meant carbon based molecule that doesn't dissolve well in water.

The National Cholesterols Education Program by the American Heart Association suggest various guidelines with relation to different stages of cholesterols,

Total Cholesterols [mg/dl]	Levels
< 200	Desirable
200 to 239	Borderline high
>240	High

- **Where does cholesterol come from?**

The liver is responsible for managing the levels of LDL in the body. It manufactures and secretes LDL into the bloodstream. There are receptors on liver cells that can "monitor" and try to adjust the LDL levels. However, if there are fewer liver cells or if they do not function effectively, the LDL level may rise.

Diet and genetics both play a factor in a person's cholesterols levels. There may be a genetic predisposition for family hypercholesterolemia (hyper = more = cholesterol + emia = blood) where the number of liver receptor cells is low and LDL levels rise causing the potential for heart disease at a younger age.

In the diet, cholesterol comes from saturated fats that are found in meats, eggs and dairy products. Excess intake can cause LDL levels in the blood to rise. Some vegetable oils made from coconut, palm and cocoa are also high in saturated fats.

Is cholesterol a steroid?

Steroids are lipids because they are hydrophobic and insoluble in water. But they do not resemble lipids since they have a structure composed of four fused rings (molecular structure). Whereas cholesterol is the most common steroid and is the precursor to vitamin-D, testosterone, estrogen, progesterone, aldosterone and bile salts.

- **Can hormone affect your muscles?**

Muscles are mostly genetically programmed. But they are also influenced by hormones such as testosterone, which makes muscles grow….. Other hormones influence muscle mass too. For example, cortisol (produced by stress) can cause muscles to atrophy if it present in high amounts for long period of time.

- **Does a steroid affect cholesterols?**

Steroids are known to significantly raise LDL levels and Lower HDL levels. Interestingly, the adverse effects anabolic steroids have on cholesterol are more common with oral forms of the drug rather than injectables.

- **Can diet provide sufficient cholesterols to develop hormone which are required to build muscles?**

Some amount of cholesterols is obtained by the body by consuming certain items in the diet portion by which the effect on the blood cholesterols level will be very less. As it is essential for formation of hormones and digestion of food, by using bile acid and vitamins, that are not soluble in water.

Few bodybuilders take steroids are also known as anabolic, androgenic steroids or just anabolic steroids. These substances are used to increase muscles mass and strength. The human body produces main hormone is testosterone.

- It has two main effects:-

Anabolic effect- promotes the build of muscles.

Androgenic effect – Promotes the development of beard, mustaches, pubic hair and deeper voice.

- **Muscles growth**

Personal trainers and fitness professionals often spend countless hours reading articles and research on new training programs and exercises ideas for developing muscular fitness. However largely because of its physiological complexity few fitness professionals are as well informed in how muscles actually adapt and grow to the progressively increasing overload demands of exercise. The intriguing cellular changes that occurs leading to muscle growth are referred to as the satellite cell theory of hypertrophy.

- **Hypertrophy**

All varieties of muscles can hypertrophy when exposed to greater stress. Hypertrophy takes place by enlargement of existing fibers, and not by formation of new fibers. Skeletal muscles hypertrophies with exercises. Cardiac muscles hypertrophies if the load on a chamber of the heart is increased for any reason. An example is the hypertrophy of muscle in the wall of the left ventricle in hypertension.

Muscle tissues in Human Body Tissue

Histology is a study that deals with tissues of human body and animals. Well if you want to brief someone about what a human body is made. We may say, head, arms, legs hands and torso or we may say our body is made up of various different types of cells.

To be more correct we can describe as how our group of cell are bounded together in an organized manner to perform certain functions. Many cells are united to create a group that is known as tissue, that later build organ and muscle to form our body parts.

Apart from muscle tissue there are different types of tissues such as

- Connective tissue
- Epithelial tissue
- Nervous tissue

Muscles Tissue

As above mentioned, as we observed there are different types of tissues which are made from cells to work together. Now we will go through the details of Muscle Tissue.

Muscles tissues are made from excitable cell. The length of the cell is elongated and full of fibers. Allowing movement in our body parts which makes us comfortably move our body is enabled because of such cells. This is also known as contraction of muscles. These cells are arranged in parallel lines to form a bundle which make the muscle tissue strong.

Force and movement of internal organs is produced through the functioning of these muscles tissues. Generally there are 3 known types –

- Visceral muscles- seen on inside layer of organs.
- Skeletal muscles- are connected along with bones which cause overall motion.
- Cardiac muscles- help the blood pump throughout the heart.

For example: take a series of rubber band and bundle them in a straight line formation. Then try to stretch them. The muscle tissue will be same replica of bundle rubber bands.

Epithelial Tissue

This tissue is made from cells which are very different from muscle tissue. Epithetical cells are columnar or plane in structure. These cells are bounded together creating a single slip. This tissue provides good protection shield to our body by means of skin. In the organs and internal cavities epithetical tissues are seen.

Connective tissues

Connective tissues are made of connective wed inside our body. These tissues hold our body part together and provide support to them is the function of tissue. Our body parts are inter-connected with this tissue. Connective tissues are made up of fibers that look like liquid, solid jelly like matrix substance which fill the spaces inside our body.

Nervous Tissue

These tissues are found in the brain system. Like electrical circuit, the nervous system sends signals from nerves to the spinal cord and brain. Cells known as neurons use these impulses, making us to use our senses.

How tissue produce hormone?

Loose connective tissue consisting of adipocytes their anatomical term is Adipose tissue or fat. The objective of these tissues is to provide cushions and padding the body and also store energy in form of fat. Adipose tissue or fat are very important for body as they contain many nerve and blood vessels which are vital for endocrine organs. We are very well aware that adipocytes main objective is to store and release energy in human body. Further most of hormones secretion in overall body is the responsibility of endocrine glands.

How the Bodybuilding Training actually Works

When you perform any exercise, with barbell or dumbbell like you imagine that you are performing shoulder exercise which specifically focuses on deltoids. But when you train shoulders it is not only the shoulder exercise but along with it there are other muscles involved while performing the exercise like for example, muscles of back, arms (triceps), etc. The point to focus and emphasize here is that you make any kind of movement whether you do bench press, shoulder press, leg press, or walking or simple breathing exercises; it involves a series of complex combinations of muscle contractions. Here to train muscles a proper technique holds the focal point to train the body and transform it in a way desired by you with planned sessions.

The working of muscle depends upon the quality of fiber (muscle fiber). These fibers have a simple function of contraction and relaxation when they are stimulated by performance of different exercises. The quality of the fibers also specifies the flexibility of the body. If the body fibers reaches to their full contraction and relaxation it is found that body muscles are flexible and if body muscles are rigid it means the fibers are not getting full contracted and relaxed. This deformity is because of lack in workout technique. How the lifting technique and body type fibers are the flexibility depends upon it.

Many years of study on bodybuilding have learned that if different exercises are performed to train muscle it will bring great visual effect. Instead of heavy weights in a single maximum lift. Bodybuilders use the techniques of less weight and do series of repetitions known as sets. They perform 4 to 6 exercises for uppers body and 6 to 8 exercises for lower body. Further each sets of repetitions 15 to 20 of different weights and various exercises for particular exercises. The exercises will be performed till the last strength. After a strenuously exercises, the particular muscles will not be trained again as it required time to recover so for 24 hours the trained muscles will not be trained again.

Training of muscles is a combination of various method and training loads to bring the desirable effects in their muscles. To know the difference of muscle fibers nature, muscle biopsies was done on bodybuilders and weight lifters, as it was noticed that, weight lifters their fibers are strong and small in number of very thick. Whereas, the bodybuilders' muscles fibers are normal in size, but very large in number. The result was surprising, from where does the extra fibers come?

It was noticed that as growth process towards adolescence it means cell multiplication. After reaching the full maturation stage it was noticed that growing new cell will be stopped and there won't be any multiplication of cells. But bodybuilding training was proven it wrong and it has made to do research and think over again on multiplication of cells and can it be implemented for others sports.

Basic Training

Every beginner bodybuilder's first task is to build concrete foundation of muscles mass not bulk or fat. Further the muscles mass is transformed into a quality muscles which is necessary for bodybuilding. This is only possible through basic hard training using heavy weights and struggling for months. Basic training meant not just few four to five exercises but thirty to forty exercises to tone up each and every part of body muscles.

In the end phase what you want is solid hard muscles mass a raw material which is necessary to build a great physique. Heredity, body composition and intensity of training help in the improvement of the body. The development of great physique faster or slower has no guaranty of defined muscles. What matters is how far you are going to push yourself.

During the beginning stage because of enthusiasm you may train daily for 4 hours and throughout the week with no rest along with not giving sufficient time for your body to recover. Most of the beginners after this stage find themselves in over trained phase and if you are still continuing with same zeal, well all it depends upon your strong mental and biochemical limitation of your body. But it is outstanding that human physiques get adjusted to the training load every time you exceed the limits by lifting heavy weights the body gets adapted to it. But at that stage lifting heavy weights is not advisable but learning the correct exercises is important.

The Basic Muscles

Body contains 600 muscles but while pursuing bodybuilding we look after only few of these. During designing bodybuilding workout pattern generally the body parts are divided into following- Lats, Deltoids, Pectorals, Legs, Biceps, Triceps and Abdomen. Considering such common body parts designing a workout pattern will not be an ideal workout pattern to develop a good bodybuilder.

When you consider arms and shoulder, these are not just single muscles to be involved in development of body part. But while developing even other muscles are included during the workout of a specific muscles like when you are doing chest workout, to perform the chest pectorals workout our shoulder, triceps and even back muscles are included, so it mean to develop a workout patterns for such complex muscles, we require a good knowledge of muscle physiology and the only we can design a sophisticated program for training. Therefore there are many subdivisions of muscles such as.

- Lastissimus and spinal erectors
- Deltoids, trapezius
- Pectorals
- Biceps, Triceps and Forearm
- Quadriceps, Hamstring and Claves
- Abdomen, Obliques

- Forearms (inside and outside)
- Claves (gastrocnemius, soleus)

If your basic training workout pattern triggers all the above mentioned body parts then you are on right path to create a good quality physique. When your physique attains the maximum improvement, then to further attain development, you need to create or focus on advance training workout.

DIET AND NUTRITION

All bodybuilders have to take care about their diet, whether they have to gain weight or lose weight well it depends upon their daily load of calories. But most common mistake of everyone is without understanding the foundation of diet and required nutrition they will be pursuing diet and later there will be adverse effects which most of the bodybuilders will not be able to understand the lack of performance after following a systematic weight training pattern and doing strict diet. Bodybuilders should understand what they want from their physique or how they want to transform their physique. It is like you are going to change your body composition to a champion form while maintaining your diet and with that you have to look after your muscle mass, strength, and flexibility intact. Therefore diet is very vital part for bodybuilders with a systematic weight training pattern.

There are many new weight training pattern which are discovered every years to develop muscles and fibers of body. Training like cross fitness, callisthenic exercises, steam and sauna bath and such many workouts and infrastructure are developed for purpose of bodybuilding. And that is the reason, every year there are many bodybuilders participating and the level of competition is becoming difficult ever year. This is only possible because of level of standard and better understanding of contents of diet which are essential to develop muscles to compete.

In bodybuilding it is always said the best method of training is to understand the diet and nutrition study. The more you know about the diet and nutrition contents the better bodybuilder you will be then others every year. But diet accompanied with hard work and dedicated training will always create a champion. It is believed that balance of training, diet and strong zeal is the key root to success in bodybuilding.

In early beginning of bodybuilding era, everyone use to follow diet according to their own instincts. The common logic of bodybuilders during that phase was during off season to gain weight sufficient without the observation that their muscle mass is getting converted into fat. Because of which they were losing their definition and proportion of their well develop bodybuilding physique. Later, bodybuilders, who toned their physique all season without getting bulked up. It was that time when everyone started realizing the importance of diet and nutrition and their role in maintaining the muscle mass. Most of the bodybuilders understand later that gaining muscle mass is very difficult then gaining weight which could be just fat size. Later again they have to cut their size to gain muscle mass during their competition season.

Once after gaining muscle mass if bodybuilders maintain that mass and add into every year. They will gain huge muscle in minimum years compare to gain bulk size and again getting ripped off. If you maintain your muscle mass year by year logically it is assume that every six months half an inch muscle size is gained. So now you can image to gain couple of inches how many years are require for a bodybuilder. Then again it depends on the genetic factor if the genetics are well improve then the gaining of muscle accelerate and the result will be noticed in few years and if genetic factors are not supportive then it may take a long time to show improvement. To be on top and to become champion, you need to keep testing your limits or challenge yourself every time. This will be only possible when your body is loaded with sufficient nutrition.

About diet and nutrition it is very simple to learn how to make use of diet for your weight gain or weight loss weight and the nutritional values which are required in diet. Every individual basis necessity of nutritional intake is different, understanding the physique and applying diet for weight gain or loss of weight is to be observed like while doing workout you will be observing whether the going on workout is putting impact of the targeted muscles or no. While doing diet also you need to be a researcher on yourself and notify the change of your physique and accordingly you have to adjust your diet.

Learning the importance of diet and nutrition is very essential for a bodybuilder. The variables which are vital play important role in construction of energy to preserve mass of muscles. Knowing various nutrition types that are useful for body is not sufficient. But you need to understand how to apply the nutrition knowledge according to your need by understanding your body type.

The Special Necessity of Diet and Nutrition of Bodybuilders

Bodybuilders requirements and demands from their physique is special than any other sports. At one time they need muscle mass with less body fat which is very difficult in present era as there are many artificial synthesized food items. This cannot be fulfilling the requirement of body to construct muscles. Sports like athletics, wrestling, boxing and gymnastics these sportsman are required to become lean, they follow a training pattern which burn their fat and also consume much calories that they don't require to maintain diet to keep down their weight nor they have any such restrictions of maintenance of body fat to minimum like bodybuilders do during their competition. Footballers mostly work on strength of muscles with very less attention to weight loss or reduction of body fat. Therefore bodybuilders, have no sign of negativity in their performance. They are required to eat sufficient amount of calories to grow and then be able to reduce body fat at the same time without losing their muscle mass. Aerobic workout help bodybuilders to burn excess calories but at the same point their gym workout shouldn't suffer. They are required to maintain calories but also need to eat sufficient protein to build and maintain muscles.

Nutrition

Protein, Carbohydrates, Fats, Vitamins, Minerals, Water are the basic nutrients which are required for body to attain sufficient growth and energy production.

Macronutrients are of three types:

1) Protein consists of various amino acids, which are used as building blocks for muscles. It is also present in all organs and helps in the development in structure of tendons, bone and skin. It is also involved in many chemical reactions which occur in body like enzymes reactions.
2) Carbohydrate is called as fuel body as it is utilized to create energy. It is made of many complex starch and sugar molecule.
3) Fat or lipids is a form of most thick pack of energy stores and are not soluble in water.

What needs to be included in diet to ensure the necessary gain of muscles should be known. After this, you just have to take care of balancing the required nutrients like how much quantity you need to have compared to the others. Let there be any type of metabolism or body composition, every physique needs a certain amount of nutrients in a specific pattern for the development of growth. The above mentioned details are very necessary to be followed to accelerate muscle development, fat metabolism to make energy.

Protein

To built, repair and maintain of muscle tissue the main nutrient is protein. In bodybuilding, to develop muscles in spite of hard training, one requires lots of protein.

The essential amino acids must be present in protein to be absorbs by body to develop muscles. If all essential amino acids are not present in protein body will not digest to improve it. Body cannot produce all essential amino acids and others essential amino acids will have to be taken from food.

To develop protein, carbon, hydrogen and oxygen are the main elements which are required along with other macronutrients and one more element which will be only present in protein is nitrogen rather than any other nutrients. Further the nitrogen is classified in positive nitrogen balance and negative nitrogen balance. Anabolic state-able to build muscle are referred as positive nitrogen balance or catabolic one-losing muscle are referred as negative nitrogen balance.

There are foods which are called as complex protein. It is so, these complex proteins provides all essential amino acids which are required for body growth like for example, meat, fish, eggs, milk, soybeans and various vegetables. The amount of protein used will be differing for these foods. For example: if food contains 20 grams protein then body may consume only 15 grams protein of the available quantity.

Following is a table which shows the percentage of proteins present in foods and actually on what percentage it will be absorbed by body to built muscle.

Food	% Protein by Weight	% Net Protein Utilization
EGGS	12	94
MILK	4	82
FISH	18-25	80
CHEESE	22-36	70
BROWN RICE	8	70
MEAT-FOWL	19-31	68
SOYBEAN FLOUE	42	62

❖ The more refined protein is whey which is derived from milk. It has more net protein then eggs

The above table explains the difference between proteins actually contains in food and how much it will be utilized by body to develop muscles.

Example: Eggs consist of 12 percent of protein. But because of few essential amino acids about 94 percent of protein will be utilized by body. Whereas soya bean has 42 percent of protein but only 62 percent of protein will be utilized by body to develop proteins.

Egg is the perfect source of protein and hence it is considered for basic comparison in rating the quality of protein with other foods.

FOOD	PROTEIN RATING
EGGS (WHOLE)	100
FISH	70
LEAN BEEF	69
COW'S MILK	60
BROWN RICE	57

RICE	56
SOYBEAN	47
WHOLE-GRAIN WHEAT	44
PEANUT	43
DRY BEAN	34
POTATO	34

The above table gives total value to eggs. The is a myth nowadays that only to eat egg white and not the yolk as it is understood that yolk contains fat and egg white doesn't. Actually yolk also contains essential proteins same as egg white.

❖ Prohibit yolk eating only if you have cholesterol problem and better consult doctor before eating yolk on daily basis.

In the above table, there are many foods which don't contain all the essential amino acids. But if you combine few foods items which after eating you will get all the essential amino acids then such diet could be very useful for muscle development.

Like it is mentioned in a book, "In Diet for a Small Planet" by Frances Moore (Ballantine Books, 1974) the following combinations are recommended:

Grains with seeds
Bread with seed meals, Bread with sesame or sunflower seed spread, Rice with sesame seeds.

Grains with milk products
Ex: Cereal with milk, Pasta with milk or cheese, Bread with milk or cheese, etc.

Grains with legumes
Ex: Rice and beans, Wheat bread and baked beans, Corn soy or wheat-soy bread, Legume soup with bread.

Protein Supplements
It is said that protein requirement for a bodybuilder is 1 gram per pound body weight per day for few individuals. But as you k now that, obtaining such heavy dose of

protein through food intake is almost impossible as the calories consumption will be more and also such food contains fats. And that is the reason as to why the food supplements are discovered. Protein supplement are cost effective and serve the purpose of exact nutrition of protein required for body and with no dietary fat.

Nowadays there are varieties of protein supplements available around. Many supplements of proteins are not just proteins but they are dense-nutrient with vitamin and mineral along with macronutrients like proteins and carbohydrate. Protein supplement which suits your diet and nutrition value could be very helpful.

There is huge selection of protein supplements which could help you to choose one. But always make sure that before selecting any protein supplement to read the nutrition facts which will be printed on the label. Because few supplements may not be just protein but they may also contain a few amounts of carbohydrates which may not fit in your diet plan. Carbohydrates if taken in excess could add extra calories to your diet and will also make difficult to burn fat. It is always better to know the amount of carbohydrate in protein supplement.

Proteins supplements are not to be taken during or with the meal. Protein should be utilized as a protein synthesis and not for energy production. It is always observed to include carbohydrate with protein supplement for good response of body or can be taken as meal replacement.

Proteins supplements are further classified into three types,

1) Milk protein 2) Egg protein and 3) Soy protein

All the protein supplements are known to be high quality proteins which are useful for development of muscles. It is better to choose one protein supplement and see the result before using any another protein supplement. Nowadays compared to milk and egg protein it is observed that soy protein supplements are attracting much attention of everyone as soya proteins reduce serum cholesterol in few individuals.

Carbohydrate

Carbohydrates are considered to be major nutrient of dietary plan and also it acts as fuel for body supplying energy to burn calorie. A carbohydrate molecule contains carbon, hydrogen and oxygen. Plants produce carbohydrate through photosynthesis by using sun energy and animal through glycogen synthesis. Glucoses mean sugar, but when sugar means it is not the table sugar which is served in daily tea or coffee. There are many different types of sugars which are connected with carbohydrates.

Monosaccharide's

Glucose (blood sugar), Fructose (fruit sugar), Galactose (a kind of milk sugar)

Oligosaccharides

Sucrose (table sugar), Lactose (milk sugar), Maltose (malt sugar)

Polysaccharides

Plant polysaccharides (starch and cellulose), Animal polysaccharides (glycogen)

The metabolism of carbohydrate to be measured is called as glycemic index. If carbohydrates are metabolized quickly then it is called as high glycemic index and if the carbohydrates are metabolized slowly then it will be considered as low glycemic index. Before simple carbs are high glycemic index (fruits processed sugar) and complex carbs are low glycemic index (starch, cellulose).

While planning diet pattern you need to be very careful about these glycemic index. As such, milk product contains low glycemic index because of fat. Whereas a kind of chinese rice, surprising has high glycemic index.

Carbohydrates are the food nutrients from for the body to convert into energy. When carbohydrates are broken through digestion they form glucose which will be circulated through blood stream and will be supplying energy to muscular contraction and later the excess glucose will be stored in muscles or liver in form of glucogen for future use.

The importance of carbohydrate for bodybuilders is of various reasons:

1. Carbohydrates stored in muscles as glycogen will supply energy during heavy weight training.
2. In the individual cells when glycogen and water is stored it will increases the muscle size.
3. Carbohydrates supply fuel to brain to perform it also monitors behavior, personality and mental ability.

Carbohydrate always supply fuel for intense training like anaerobic, short interval session, intense blast of energy and ability to sustain the training during deficiency of oxygen. It will be carbohydrates which will be supplying energy whenever there is intense weight training or 100 mtrs sprint.

Carbohydrate Supplements

Body needs glycogen and amino acids whenever intense training is demanded. Carbohydrates are very essential to be in body after intense workout or to maintain the energy requirement body will start using the amino acids and thus there will be cut down of muscle size. After finishing workout body will be in need of high demands of nutrients. In fact, for best result after finishing the workout within 20 minutes body must be loaded with carbohydrates.

This happens because most of the bodybuilders after workout prefer to do aerobic workout like, using treadmill, stepper or cycling that time the body will be in need of carbohydrate or else body will start metabolizing amino acids to supply energy for the workout.

Dietary Fats

Fats are the solid form of macronutrients available in our body. Fat function is to supplement energy and is also known as reserved energy. Fats are formed from three elements carbon, hydrogen and oxygen. But the way the atoms are interlinked together is different. Oils are also known as simple fats and it is in form of liquid rather solid at room temperature. On the contrary, the fats that is found in animals and plants, are insoluble in water. The fat is divided into three categories in simple fat (triglycerids) compound fats (phospholipids, glucolipids, lipoproteins) and derived fats (cholesterol).

The functions of fats are,

1) They serve as major source of energy storage in our body.
2) They protect and provide cushioning to our vital organs during the time of impact.
3) During extreme cold, fats produce heat and protect our body, they act as insulator for our body

During intense workout like aerobic the body uses fat and carbohydrate on 50-50 basis to produce energy. If the intensity of workout is consistent for longer time then the utilization of fat will be higher. If the workout prolongs for more than three hours, the percentage of burning fat into energy will be more than 80 percent.

The biochemical composition of fat molecules will differ for saturated, unsaturated and polyunsaturated. These three compositions of fat only differ by the number of hydrogen atoms that are attach to the molecules.

Saturated Fats are straight lines like cord in a badly tangled mess. And un-saturated fats are like string with not many knots. And the poly-unsaturated fats are like encircled string without any tangles. If in body there is more saturated fat then there will be clogs in the arteries and which may result in risk of heart attack. If in daily diet saturated fat intake is high then there are chances of raised level of cholesterol in the blood. It is so, because doctors advise two-third of fat consumption in diet must be poly-unsaturated fat.

Following food items of various fat compositions:

Saturated Fats

Lamb, Chicken, Shell Fish, Egg yolk, Cream, Beef, Pork, Milk

Butter, Chocolate, Lard

Unsaturated Fats

Avocados, Cashews, Olives and olive oil, Peanuts, peanut oil and peanut butter

Polyunsaturated fats

Almonds, Cottonseed oil, Margarine (usually), Pecans, Sunflower oil, Corn oil, Fish, Mayonnaise, Safflower oil, Soybean oil, Walnuts

Bodybuilders require essential fatty acids

In daily diet even fats are essential nutrient. Today's bodybuilders prefer to do low fat diet because they should not develop fat or load excess calories. Foods and supplements now are in markets which are accessible with all the essential good fat

Fish oil, polyunsaturated vegetable oil, MCTs (medium chain triglycerids), monounsaturated fats, fatty acid supplements.

Fish oil

Fish like salmon, trout or mackerel must be included in our diet. Because fish fats are not produced by our body it is required to be taken externally through fish food. The fish oil is necessary for organs and especially for our brain. Fish oil will be also available in form of food supplements.

Polyunsaturated vegetable oil

There are two type of oil in this category i.e. linoleic and linolenic acids. Oils of sunflower, corn, safflower cannot produce linolenic acids. Linolenic acid is produced only by soybean oil which is available in supermarket. Linolenic acid is an important component of flaxseed oil which can be extracted from walnuts and pumpkin seeds.

MCTs (Medium Chain Triglycerides)

MCTs can be acquired from common coconut oil. There is a belief in bodybuilding about MCTs that it wills not deposit fat cells. But the updated study on MCTs has shown that the belief is incorrect. MCTs don't give any strength, size, speed or stamina to athlete. They are just fat calories.

Monounsaturated fats

These fats are most essential fat to our body. They don't affect on cholesterol or any regular hormonal action like poly-unsaturated fats. These fats are noticed in olive oil and macadamia nuts.

Fatty Acid Supplement

There are variety of fish oil and other related supplements in the market which contain essential fatty acids.

Water

Our body's major component is water and is the essential nutrient to regulate our body temperature. It plays vital role in for carrying different chemicals in the body and is also medium in which many different bio-chemical reactions take place among the basic nutrients.

Body consists of 40 to 60 percent of H_20. Muscles consists 72 % of water by weight and fat weight is only 20 to 25 %. When excessive fluid is not included in regular diet, or any activities, it will have a direct impact of size of muscles. If water is not taken in sufficient quantity in a day then body will be dehydrated and body will begin to protect by retaining the water in subcutaneous tissue. This will smooth the muscular definition.

The stored water will get contaminated and because of dehydration kidneys can't filter contaminated water properly. Further with the help of liver these waste products will be processed. Such interference with the main function of body will results in breakdown of fat. And that is the reason without adequate water in b0dy you are likely to end up water-logged, bloated and obese. This procedure is catastrophic for a bodybuilder to maintain his body definition.

In dehydration, sodium can't be removed from the body and because of this water retention occurs and if again sodium is added to your diet. It will simply make the problem crucial.

Bodybuilders have to drink lots of water as they perform intense weight training. There is no substitution for water, so don't count it.

Vitamins

Vitamins are organic substance and they act as catalysts substances that help to trigger other reactions in our body. Vitamins don't contribute in supplying energy or develop muscles mass. The body requires vitamins in a minute quantity and that will be gained through our daily food. Vitamins can be classified into 02 categories water soluble vitamin and fat soluble vitamin.

❖ Water Soluble Vitamins:

These vitamins are not stored in the body and if found in excess are flushed through urine. On daily basis it is necessary to take water soluble vitamins.

Water soluble vitamins are:

B1 (thiamin), B2 (riboflavin), B3 (niacin, nicotinic, nicotinamide)

B5 (pantothenic acid), B6 (pyridoxine), B12 (cyanocobalamin)

Biotin, Folate (folic acid, folacin), Vitamin C (ascorbic acid)

Vitamin A (retinol)

❖ Fat Soluble Vitamins:

These vitamins are stored in the fatty tissues of the body. On daily basis it is not necessary to take fat soluble vitamins.

fat soluble vitamins are:

Vitamin A, Vitamin D, Vitamin E, Vitamin K

Minerals

These are in-organic substance and requirement of body for these elements is in small quantity. The total body weight about four percent is of these twenty two metallic elements. Minerals are present in water and soil. The root absorbed the minerals from the soil which nourishes the plants and human eat plants and animals they get minerals which are needs there physiques to grow. If we consume different types of vegetables and meats then we get sufficient amount of minerals.

Minerals have an important role in variety of metabolic process and plays vital part in fusion of chemical mixture like glycogen, protein and fats.

Below is the brief direction of basic requirements of minerals for our body:

Calcium: It strengthens our teeth and bones. Calcium is found in milk products vegetables, mustard greens, seafood and oysters. Calcium deficiency can cause muscular cramps and osteoporosis.

RDA: 1200 mg males of 11 to 24 age and 800 mg in males over 25 ages.

Phosphorous: It is present in every cell of the body consisting DNA, RNA and ATP. Phosphorous can be noticed in whole grains, egg yolks, meat, milk, fish, chicken. Phosphorous is important to regulate the pH (acidity/alkalinity) level in our body.

RDA: 1200 mg males of 11 to 24 age and 800 mg in males over 25 ages.

Magnesium: It will be all over in our body. It is an initiator of enzymes involving in nearly all course of action in body. Magnesium is containing in whole grains, nuts, non vegetarian, and chocolate.

RDA: 400 mg males of 15 to 18 age and 350 mg in males over 19 ages.

Sodium: It regulates the levels of fluids in the body. It is also occupied in muscular retrenchment. Sodium is obtainable in common table salt and nearly all of the fruits, animal foods, seafood, milk and eggs. If sodium level is increased, it elevates water retention and sugar level in blood. If there is sodium deficiency it causes muscular weakness and cramps.

RDA: 1,100 to 3.300 mg

Chlorine: It is essential for digestive juice and act with combination of sodium. It is present in table salt, meat, seafood, eggs, milk.

RDA: 1700 to 5100 mg

Potassium: It is used in metabolism of protein and carbohydrate. Potassium combined with sodium to function inside cell to be in charge of liquid osmosis. It is present in meat, milk, cereals and vegetables. If there is potassium deficiency it causes muscular weakness and if it is in excess quantity it causes vomiting.

RDA: 1,875 to 5,625 mg

Sulfur: It is considered necessary for amalgamation of necessary metabolites. It is present in protein foods like milk, eggs, cheese, legumes and meat

RDA: not advised

Additional minerals are also significant for our growth but at minimum contain on daily. These are

Iron, Zinc, Copper, Iodine, Manganese, Fluoride, Molybdenum

Cobalt, Selenium, Chromium

There are other essential minerals required for the body but for them no daily recommended amount is specified.

Tin, Nickel, Vanadium, Silicon

Vitamin and Mineral Supplements

Through our daily intake many of us feel that we are not getting adequate amount of vitamins and minerals. There are a number of causes for the same, including which manner the food is grown, how it is processed and in the manner it is distributed. But this is also a fact that, intense workout increases our requirement for vitamin and mineral of all types.

In the earlier phase of bodybuilding, there were no experts who could recommend the exact amount of vitamin and minerals which were necessary for body. Most of the bodybuilders used to experiment on themselves by witnessing the changes in their energy, endurance, ability to train harder or to recover and in muscular definition or size.

But nowadays, all types of supplements are available in health store, but can also get supplement of daily pack with the right amount of each mineral and vitamin with correct balance.

Only to worry is about the over dose. Vitamin and minerals are required in body at a very less amount to do their functions. Latest study shown that supplement can be very beneficial to prevent number of diseases. But if they are taken in large amount adverse side effects may occur.

Purpose of study:

The study is about finding the development of muscles in endomorphs type bodybuilders based on the level of HDL and LDL; and the variation in muscle mass because of diet and weight training patterns in male bodybuilders. The study will also focus on the finding of lipoprotein profile of endomorph bodybuilders during the off season and competition season by monitoring their diet and providing them weight training pattern. The study will also notice the different types of foods items which are suitable for diet and specific exercises for weight training patterns. Nutritional intake is restricted and the body builders consume a high-protein, low-fat, moderate-carbohydrate diet before the competition. Calorie intake is made twice of fat and carbohydrate is increased approximately tenfold after competition. In outline, the body-builders practiced dedicated dietary control while getting ready for a competition when the event is over they consume with high calorie and fat intake. This may result in heavy loss of muscle mass after the competition and gain before the competition. These changes in diet and weight may be contributed in drastic changes in HDL and LDL profile in body builders.

STATEMENT OF THE PROBLEM:

The principle of this learning is to evaluate the levels of HDL and LDL and whether HDL and LDL contribute towards in development of muscles; and effect of variation in muscle mass because of diet and weight training during and after their body building competition.

Problem Definition:

1) Most of the beginner weight trainees will not be aware of their body type before choosing bodybuilding as profession.

2) High Density Lipoproteins and Low Density Lipoproteins are helpful in development of muscles.

3) Orthodox gym instructors

4) Diet pattern

5) Weight training pattern

OBJECTIVE OF STUDY:

The study aims to find out the levels of High Density Lipoproteins (HDL) and Low Density Lipoproteins (LDL) which are helpful in the development of muscles in bodybuilders with a focal concentration on their weight training method and diet pattern.

HYPOTHESIS

1. It is hypothesized that, finding the levels of HDL (High Density Lipoproteins) and LDL (Low Density Lipoproteins) are related in development of muscles in body builders.
2. It is hypothesized that, variation in lipoprotein (HDL and LDL) are responsible for the variations in muscles mass and helpful in development of muscles in bodybuilders.
3. It is hypothesized that, there exists a significance variation in the Subject & Control Group with HDL readings during Competition Phase.
4. It is hypothesized that, there is no significant variation in Subject and Control Group with LDL readings during Competition Phase.
5. It is hypothesized that, there is no significant variation between the Subject & Control Group, with HDL readings during off-Season Phase.
6. It is hypothesized that there is no significant difference between the Subject and Control Group with LDL readings during off-Season Phase.

Limitation:

1) Body builders may change their diet pattern and weight training method without informing the researcher.

2) Subjects may use food supplement which are not prescribed or may use enhancing substances and steroids to increase their level of performance.

Delimitation:

1) Biochemical test will be accurate.

2) Levels of HDL and LDL will be understood which are necessary for muscle building will be achieved.

3) Effect of diet and weight training on HDL and LDL levels on muscle mass will be ascertained.

4) On the levels of HDL and LDL it can also be used for various tests like doping.

5) Will also come to know which lipo-protein is necessary for development of hormone which is used for improvement of muscles.

6) National Level endomorph bodybuilders are selected for subject group based on the characteristic of endomorph type body.

7) Direct Enzymatic Calorimetric Method will be used on blood samples to detect the levels of HDL and LDL.

Definition of importance terms used in the study:

Bodybuilding: A sports involving strenuous physical exercises in order to strengthen and enlarge the muscles of the body.

Weight training: A physical training that involves lifting weights to improve fitness.

Diet: A special course of food to which a person restrict themselves for various reasons like weight lose, weight gain or muscle gain.

High Density Lipoprotein (HDL): It is considered as Good Cholesterol because it takes cholesterol from artery to liver and does not allow plaque to form in the walls of artery.

Low Density Lipoprotein (LDL): It is considered as Bad Cholesterol because it takes cholesterol from liver and deposits them in the walls of artery which is called as plaque.

Signification of the Study:

1) Through this research I would like to analyze the contribution of HDL and LDL in the development of muscles in endomorphs bodybuilders.
2) On base of LDL & HDL readings, the test can also be used by NADO, IOC, IPC and WADA for doping.
3) If HDL and LDL data is studied with insulin data, there is much scope for study related to overweight/obesity problems and maintenance of fitness.
4) This research may also explain why few bodybuilders died or dying because of cardiac arrest while performing on the stage during competition.
5) The study also serves to be useful in dealing with the aging phenomena related with muscles loss.
6) Study will also show why steroids are taken by bodybuilders.

CHAPTER II

REVIEW OF RELATED LITERATURE

The study is based on the main factors of the influence of diet and weight training on HDL and LDL levels of endomorph type bodybuilders. the hypothesis was formulated; the limitation of the study and delimitation are also explained including operational definitions.

Now, the literature on the similar topic or subject will be review based on the earlier studies with specific reference. In this chapter, the review of related literature is presented.

In 1940, Sheldon proposed a theory about how there are certain body types that are associated with certain personality characteristics. he claimed that there are 3 such somato-types People those who are interested to join gym and are willing to develop muscles or to lose weights. They will be inundated with the different types of training patterns, food supplements, diets and information on these items out there. There were many questions about diet and weight training patterns in their mind and they used to get different responses from each bodybuilders or gym coaches or trainers. They had no idea what they had to do. The resultant of my status was about 6 months in the gym with little improved body and almost no motivation with confused workout patterns. They used to follow anyone whom they used to find a good bodybuilder.

Because of such misguidance they will be completely discouraged by their decision and thought of giving up muscle building. Well then when someone suggests them to read articles, magazine and books on body types and on framing suitable weight training pattern.

After reading related books on bodybuilding they understood the importance of body types and how the muscles gaining phenomenon is different for different body types.

After having conversations with many experts, discussing with friends, gym instructors and bodybuilders every beginner will be again at the initial point to understanding the difference of body types.

Somato stratification:

No two individuals are alike. Each individual differ from the other individual. Many superior authorities study the differences of the body built and classified them into different types by estimating the relative predominance of inherited characteristics namely bones, muscles development and fat distribution. This is called somato stratification. The classification made by Kretschmer and Sheldon are more popular in the field of physical education.

Sheldon classification of somato types:-

Sheldon classified body by utilizing three body components designated as,

1) Endomorph
2) Mesomorph and
3) Ectomorph.

The components are named after three embryonic layers. They are:
 1) endoderm- inner layer
 2) mesoderm- middle layer
3) ectoderm- outer layer.
An individual's somato type endomorphy, mesomorphy and ectomorphy rating scale is from 1 to 7 on each component. Thus 7-1-1 would be the designation assigned to an extreme endomorph. A 1-7-1 would be extreme mesomorph and 1-1-7 an extreme ectomorph.

There are different types of necessity training patterns and diet plans. It has been listed that there are 03 body types: Ecto-morphs, Meso-morphs and Endo-morphs with specific characteristic.

Simon & Schuster (1985), "Encyclopedia of Modern Bodybuilding", on Arnold Schwarzenegger, New York, The details of endomorphs body types are as mentioned, Endomorphs body types are soft in muscles and they gain fat very easy. They have thick arms and legs. They have solid muscles on the lower body. And reasons they will develop define and huge legs through workouts like squat. Endomorph will not have much difficulty in development of muscles. What concern of such body type is how to lose fat and weight! Also they have to be very careful about their calorie intake so they should not gain fat or become over weight. A little variation in diet will make them gain weight rapidly. This shows that, they have slow metabolic rate. And because of this such body type has to do their daily physical activity and also watch diet careful to gain or maintain their muscles mass.

Specification of Endomorph:

- Need to work hard to lose fat
- Gain muscles
- Also gain fat very easily
- Round physique
- Definition of muscles is not so well
- Soft and round body
- Bone structure strong
- Long limbs
- Strong

The following tips for Endomorphs body type will be beneficial:

- To burn fat they need to add high set and repetitions with minimum rest time
- Swimming, dance, cycling, running, rowing such aerobic are necessary because of which consumption of calorie will take.
- Balanced nutrition with low calorie diet will be helpful to develop muscles. The calories shouldn't be negligible but minimum quantity of carbohydrate, Protein and fat with required body necessity of vitamin and mineral are essential nutrition.

Endomorph signification: - These types of people posses a lot of weight to carry and this has been proved to be a severe handicap that indulges during physical activities. Generally endomorphs are unsuccessful in gymnastic and other activities, requiring speed, agility or endurance such as running and jumping. They may be successful in golf, archery, throwing events and strength are conducive to outstanding physical performance.

Gain weight is not a problem for endomorphs body type but the disadvantage is the large amount of weight gain by such body types will be fat. To maintain the lean muscle mass endomorphs are required to train hard and burn their calories. Because of continues efforts most of the endomorphs bodybuilders such doing weight training as for the long interval of time there will not be any sign of improvement in them or the rate of improvement is very slow. Further, because of large frame and huge body structure if they continuous do weight train for long interval of time, there are also chances of joint injuries because of friction of bone in shoulder, back, knees. This lack of motivation set them back from achieving their go.

Charge and Rudnicki 2004 proposed a theory on treating to the muscle: triggering the satellite cells

Muscles are trained vigorously through weight training where there is disturbance to the muscle fibers that is referred to as muscle injury or damage in scientific investigation. This disruption to muscle cell organelles activates satellite cells, which are located on the outside of the muscle fibers between basal lamina (basement membrane) and the plasma membrane (sarcolemma) of muscles fibers to proliferate (look after and recover) to the injury site.

Of site, during biological mechanism the replacement and repair of burned muscle fibers in concern with satellite cells fusion to muscles fiber's this mechanism will lead to cross section of muscle fiber's stage called hypertrophy. Satellite cells consist of one nucleus and the duplicate nucleus can be prepared by dividing it. Further multiply of cells take place few will remain as organelles on the muscles and many will differentials and fuse with fibers to create new protein stands or myofibrils or repair damaged fibers.

Myofibrils will enlarge in width and figure. Few satellite cells after the fusion will be source of new nuclei to help the growth of muscle fibers and with these new nuclei the muscle fibers will make protein and create many contractile myofilaments called a myosin and actins in the skeletal muscle cells. Its amaze to acknowledge that many satellite cells are found with slow twitch fibers then fast twitch fibers in same muscle because they will be going through cell maintenance repair mechanism.

'Charge and Rudnicki (2004)' Growth factor theory, hormones that activate the satellite cells are fabricated to increases the size of muscle fibers. The satellite cell activity is controlled the effect of muscle growth. The main controller of these cells is Hepatocyte Growth Factor (HGF). It is proved that this factor is active in damaged muscle and responsible for creating satellite cells to transfer to damage muscle area.

'Charge and Rudnicki; (2004)' studied "fibroblast growth factor" (FGF) while doing exercise FGF is another main growth factor in muscle repair. During muscle regeneration formation of new blood capillaries is the job of FGF.

The study on insulin-like growth factor-I and –II (IGFs) has put lime light on the task of muscle growth. To improve muscle cell repair and production of protein in the DNA (Deoxy Ribo Nucelic Acid) is the vital task of IGF's.

In the consumption of protein and smoothen the progress of the entry of glucose into cell, insulin helps the procedure for muscle growth. Whereas glucose is used for intra-muscular power requirement and satellite cells use glucose as a fuel.

For muscle growth, growth hormone (GH) very much accepted for muscle growth. While doing resistance training the growth hormone is released by anterior pituitary gland when the intensity of exercise is very intense. During the muscle growth mechanism the energy is released when GH target fat metabolism. Even GH job is to convert amino acids to protein skeletal muscle.

Recent study informs that, 'testosterone' also affects muscle hypertrophy. The boosting of cellular amino acid absorption and production of protein can be done by this hormone which is similar to GH developed in pituitary gland; the neuro-transmitters which are present in the fiber are increased in number with the help of this hormone. As a steroid hormone, testosterone is a steroid hormone which can react with nuclear receptors on the DNA follow-on in protein synthesis. To regulate satellite cells at some extend are also affected by testosterone.

[Muscle Growth: The 'Bigger' Picture by 'Rasmussen and Phillips', (2003)]

Most of the related study gives us a clear picture that muscle improvement is a complicated molecular biological cell phenomenon linking the interchange of many cellular organelles and GH take place during the progress of resistance training.

For the educationist there is main purpose needs to be understood. Every time when there is rate of muscle protein production is more than the rate of muscle protein breakdown this will led to muscle growth. The production and breakdown of protein is monitored by cellular mechanism.

Muscle hyper-trophy stage can be occurred by doing resistance training and the follow-on will be increase in strength. On the other hand the duration of hyper-trophy condition is comparatively slow. To come out from his condition it will take several days or months. It is more interesting that a limited period of workout can raise the productivity of protein in two to four hours when the workout is over of which the effect will be remained until twenty four hours. If few more research is done on this topic, the discoveries may be cooperative to grab the focus of fitness people.

Men and women react in the same manner to weight training it is proved in most of the studies. In spite of gender difference in size and composition of body, even in levels of hormone, on the basis of this variation the effect of amount of hyper-trophy. As the individual keep the consistence in training the more huge and massive muscle mass will be developed then compare to beginning of the training program.

There will be decreased in the actual muscle mass due to change in mediate cellular which is due to aging. "Sarcopenia" is the phase which is referred as loss of muscle mass. The most happening news is that, if regular weight training is done it can restrict the symptoms of aging which we can say as "Anti Aging". The chief concept to know here is weight training helps to recover the stiffness connective tissue which will be around the muscle and thus it would protect from getting injured and also help in rehab therapies.

["Foss and Ketyain"] (1998) Study on Heredity that differentiates the percentage and amount of the two markedly different fiber types.

Red, tonic, Type I, slow twitch (ST) or slow-oxis=dative (SO) fibers are found in humans in the cardiovascular-type fibers have at different times. On the other side, White, phasic, Type II, fast-twitch (FT), or fast-glycolytic (FC) fibers are anaerobic type fibers. A further subdivision of Type II fibers is the IIa (fast-oxidative-glycolytic) and IIb (fast-glycolytic) fibers.

It is commendable to talk about the soleus, a muscle occupied in standing posture and way of walking, generally contains 25 to 40% more Type I fibers, while the triceps has 10 to 30% more Type II fibers than the other arm muscles. In adults the quantity and types of muscles differ to a greater extent. The latest introduction of workout pattern for daily exercises routine which consist of light, medium and intense workout training periodization are adequately give the fibers types a feeling of hypertrophy and also help in the productivity of protein creation in the body,

Wile Ford (1968) suggested that for weight training it is extremely necessary that the relation between physical fitness, dimensions of the personality and performance through physical activities is to be considered on priority during the training sessions. This is so, because the physical fitness brings about immense stability in an individual that ultimately leads to better performances.

Uppal and Sood (1988) have said that only the fittest of the fit can are excellent performers and winners. As the key role here, is played by endurance and keep going attitude that could be built up only through physical fitness. May it be athletes, bodybuilders or any other sports freaks, the motive behind their success when inquired, is the stamina that they have obtain and the level of health that is been achieved, is the key that they have expressed.

Barrow (1973) has stated that physical is the end result of m0t0r fitness, as the readiness 0f the physical being to perform heavy physical activity such as the weight training exercises, without any fatigue, or staying on even with fatigue, to build big musculature, within a pre decided period of time, is greatly dependent on the level of stamina and endurance that an individual beholds.

Cofer and Johnson (1960) have termed the sports achievers and champions to belong to a breed that is special of its kind, because the resistance power that they possess over the time is unbeatable and requires efforts of the hardest level that they have sustained to achieve it. Apart from the efforts that they put in, the nature of body that they possess is nevertheless a gift from nature that they have received. Therefore the most required physical fitness for any sports is achieved through various physical exercises. These physical exercises enhance the physical fitness by means of various factors that stimulate it, such as the breathing pattern, physical efforts, body response , intake of oxygen, resistance power of the body to face extreme weather conditions during the practice sessions, heart beat regulation, blood circulation, etc. The mastery over all these influencing factors results in overall physical fitness of the body.

Supplement consumption in bodybuilder athletes:

In a study by kern et al, since 1856 such evidence that supplements and power enhancers are regularly used by most of the sports personalities in different sports discipline. It was noticed that beta-alanine supplement possibly will progress the work out shown for the duration of a competition. 'Stout et al', was become aware of taking a serve of power drink before workout will encourage the constructive alteration of chronic exercises on body posture, cardio respiratory and stamina presentation in sports personalities. The study done by [Ziegenfuss et al], observed that fragile supplement with a product enclosed with first and foremost beta alanine, arginine, creatine malate and glycerol monostearate pump up strength not including unconstructively distressing complete hemodynamic.

 Studies with the following, non ethical aspects of muscle booster agent are used more than many decades, since '1910', when "Alkaloid" structure was created these supplements. These illegal supplement were widespread was observed among European professional athletes. In 1960 Olympic Games few deaths of athletes took place because of overdose of amphetamine.

'In 1968', Winter Olympic games in France, recognized standard laboratory tests was implemented as a practices to avoid known as "Doping". Such aggression enhancers substance were used during World War II on German soldiers to stimulate and modify their aggrieve behavior. "International Olympic Committee" has distinct "Doping" to use such any physiologic material in abnormal amount by athletes just to amplify their sportive recital in their tournament. Many studies have shown, athletes from different sports discipline are more or a smaller amount prone to "Doping" as power lifters and skaters due to all physical, mental and moral side effects, 'International Olympic Committee (IOC)', 'United States Olympic Committee (USOC)' and many other sports committees has made several legal rules to forbid "Doping". In spite of higher education on health were all positive related to supplement use. Despite plenty of information on these supplements usage few countries like Iran lack such the knowledge about illegal substances supplements. This is particularly related for bodybuilders were found using these supplements to use as every youth of Iran has a desire to become a bodybuilder. As nowadays supplements are available to everyone and bodybuilders are using it to gain muscle. The aim of study is to estimate the prevalence and determinants the use of supplements among bodybuilders of Isfahan.

['JAMA' The Journal of the American Medical Association 252(4):507-13 August 1984 (HighDensityLipoprotein Cholesterol in Bodybuilders v Powerlifters: Negative Effects of Androgen Use)]

To identify the property of erogenic substance, to find out the association between, lipid profiles and type of weight training on bodybuilders and powerlifters - The sample chosen are of same age, body fat and testosterone levels were studied before and after androgen use. Before androgen administration powerlifters had lower levels of plasma high-density-lipoprotein cholesterol (HDL-C) and HDL2-C (38 +/- 2; 6 +/- 1 mg/dl; means +/- SE, n = 8) than bodybuilders (55 +/- 2; 12 +/- 1 mg/dl; n = 8) and runners of comparable age and body fat (47 +/- 2; 14 +/- 2 mg/dl; n = 8), while levels of low-density-lipoprotein cholesterol (LDL-C) were higher in power-lifters (138 +/- 10 mg/dl) than in bodybuilders (104 +/- 7 mg/dl) and runners (110 +/- 6 mg/dl). Therefore, power-lifters had higher LDL-C/HDL-C rati0s (3.7 +/- 0.3) than bodybuilders (2.0 +/- 0.2) and runners (2.4 +/- 0.2). Androgen use by eight bodybuilders and four power-lifters lowered values of both HDL-C and HDL2-C by 55% and raised values of LDL-C (61% +/- 10%) and LDL-C/HDL-C ratios (28% +/- 40%). Therefore, the program treatment of bodybuilders is considered to be more favorable lipid profile than the program treatment used by power lifters. It is detected there is risk of coronary disease in strength trained athletes those who use androgen.

'Stefan M Pasiakos Harris R Lieberman Victor L Fulgoni, 03 "The Journal of Nutrition" Volume 145, Issue 03, March 2015, Pages 605–614 (Higher-Protein Diet are related with 2.2 Higher HDL Cholesterol and Lower BMI and Waist Circumference in US Adults) Protein consumptions above the RDA calms to cardio-metabolic risk in overweight and obese adults during weight reduction. Still the cardio-metabolic consequences of taking higher-protein diet in free-living adults have not been determined.

This research is to find out the routine protein intake [g/kg body weight (BW)] pattern stratified by weight status and their relationship with cardio-metabolic risk using data from the NHANES, 2001–2010 ($n = 23{,}876$ adults ≥ 19 y of age)

The protein intake of Americans is excess of the RDA. Higher protein diets are related with lower BMI and waist circumference and higher HDL cholesterol compared to protein intakes at RDA levels. It is found that Americans intake of daily protein is between 1.0 and 1.5 g/kg BW possibly reduces the risk of developing cardio-metabolic disease.

[The Journal of sports medicine and physical fitness 38(3):245-52 October 1998 (Effect of a pre-competition bodybuilding diet and training regimen on body composition and blood chemistry)]

This study was determined to purpose the ten week pre-competition training and diet on bodybuilders the analysis was based on blood chemistry and body composition. A adult bodybuilder who is preparing for competition first time and free from drug and steroid is free is selected to pursue the research. The calorie taken by the bodybuilder for the daily diet is 2263 cal consisting of 71% protein, 16% carbohydrate and 13% fat. The protein is as per the calculation 5.0 gm/kg. The initial weight of 76.3 kg with 16% body fat and after the intense workout the body weight is reduced to 63.4 kg with 4.4 % of body fat. It has be analysis through blood samples for amylase, TP, LDL-C, UA, TG, Alb, bilirubin and electrolytes were within the range. The levels of HDL-C is raised from 65 to 89 mg/dl-1 and the level of glucose is decreased i.e. [<50 mg/dl-1] indicating the stage of hypoglycemia. The training was intense as the levels of CK, Mg and LD were raised. Body will develop lactic acidosis which is known by the increased range of inorganic phosphorus from 3.7 to 8.2 mg/dl-1. The level of BUN (blood Urine and Nitrogen) is also above the normal range 16 to 53 mg/dl-1 and increase in level of creatine 1.1 to 1.8 mg/dl-1 may be the reason because of high protein in diet. Muscle enzyme (CK-MB) was not elevated. During pre-competition diet and training it is suggested adequate nutrition be ensured and caution taken that to avoid excessive physiologic stresses on the body to note the significant changes in body composition and blood chemistry.

How can weight training help to lower bad cholesterol?

Through the blood stream the molecules of low density lipoproteins cholesterols are transported in body tissues. There will be increases in risk of atherosclerosis if the quantity of LDL is in more in the blood. The problem of atherosclerosis starts with an injury to arterial wall that build up into a place for particles in the blood to stick. The LDL cholesterol sticks to the injured arterial walls and is oxidized. If LDL formation of particles is continued for longer interval of time then this will resultant into calcified plaque which can later be the reason of cardiac problems, heart attack or stroke, the American Heart Association says if a training program including weight training is design properly for such patient suffering with such problem with cholesterol reducing diet pattern then it will be much helpful to control LDL cholesterol levels.

Normal Levels:

If the LDL cholesterol levels are best if the range is within 100 mg/dl. "American Heart Association", has instructed about the different range of levels of LDL accordingly, if the level is in between 100 to 129 mg/dL are just above ideal, 130 to 159 mg/dL are borderline, 160 to 189 mg/dL are high and if the level is greater than 190 mg/dL are considered to be very high. It is directed by the American Heart Association that there will be greater risk for developing the atherosclerosis if the LDL cholesterol are very high.

LDL i.e. bad cholesterol can be reduced by doing weight training. In the year 1987, I.H. Ullrich and colleagues published a study conducted by HDL and LDL cholesterol levels can benefit from weight training in the "Southern Medical Journal,". The study was conducted on 25 men who weight trained for 08 weeks on every alternate day of each week. The result has shown a reduction in LDL levels in the blood stream.

Causes

When the weight training is given the reason how the mechanism exactly helps to reduce the LDL range is not understood. Perhaps due to weight training workout on body composition and the resistance training program may help to decrease the levels of LDL cholesterol. As the weight training is continued it will increase the strength and skeletal muscle growth this will promote lean body mass and reduce body fat which is one of the best health benefits required to improve the lipid profile and lower the LDL cholesterol.

Exercise Program

A weight training program must be included in the exercise program in view to increase health and fitness goals this is according to American College of Sports Medicine. At least 24 hours' rest between sessions resistance exercises can be done 2 to 3 days per week. By target all of the major muscle groups of the body around 08 to 10 exercises should be done with performing the exercises of 10 to 15 repetitions of 3 sets. It is advised that if 3 patterns of resistance training with cardiovascular exercise and a healthful diet is followed it will likely to reduce weight in few days. By losing just 5 % of body fat can improve cardiovascular health and cholesterol level.

['Jeferson Luis da Silva' 'Raul Cavalcante Maranhao' 'Carmen Guilherme Christiano de Matos Vinagre Rev Bras Med Esporte vol.16 no.1 Niterói Jan/Feb. 2010 (Effects of resistance training on low density lipoprotein)]

The motto of this review was to find whether weight training (RT) promotes any improvement on low density lipoprotein cholesterol. Important differences were observed in research protocols, making it difficult to define the benefits of RT in this review. The selection of the perfect exercise may be more beneficial for individuals with specific diseases and associated pathologies. It was determined that RT may be ideal in lowering the LDL-C levels mainly in adult men and women, in patients with diabetes mellitus type 01 and type 02 and in pre-menopausal women, not presenting differences in the elderly population. At the end the review is concluded, that the RT is a good option for physical exercise for individuals, especially when the aerobic training (AT) is contra-indicated.

[Biological, Psychological and Socio-cultural Factors Contributing to the Drive for Muscularity in Weight-Training Men (Schneider et al, 2016)]:

In 2011 Boyda and Shevlin examined MD symptoms in a sample of male bodybuilders. They identified the relationship between childhood victimization such as verbal, physical, and social bullying and MD. It was argued, that regular critique and emotional victimization by parents (Lamanna et al, 2010) and peers (Boyda and Shevlin, 2011) may lead to body image distortion and higher degrees of body dissatisfaction which, according to other studies (Pritchard et al., 2011; Mustapic et al, 2015), are related to drive for muscularity. More generally, it was found that negative appearance-based comments were associated with higher body dissatisfaction and higher driver for muscularity (Nowell and Ricciardelli, 2008). In a sample of bodybuilders childhood bullying experience were associated with higher scores in MD (Wolke and Sapouna, 2008)".

{Changes in body composition, diet, and strength of bodybuilders during the 12 weeks prior to competition (Bamman et al, 1993) "The purpose of this study was to monitor body composition, diet, and strength in male bodybuilders}

The study was conducted before 12 weeks prior to competition. The data collected the pre-competition practices were showing the effect in reducing subcutaneous fat preserved in the body while maintaining muscle mass. The study was concluded with the remarks stating, onset of the pre-competition phase resulted in strength loss

Case Study: [The Effect of 32 Weeks of Figure-Contest Preparation on a Self-Proclaimed Drug-free Female's Lean Body and Bone Mass (Petrizzo et al, 2017)]

"In the details of the study, in training for a figure competition a self-proclaimed drug-free female accomplish the low body-fat percentage essential for victory in competition without reducing the lean mass or bone density by pursuing a 32-week preparatory exercise and nutritional schedule".

Cases study by (Robinson et al, 2015) a nutrition and conditioning intervention for natural bodybuilding contest preparation.

"This interference shows that a structured and scientifically supported nutrition strategy can be applicable to get better result of the parameters significant to bodybuilding competition and prominently the health of competitors, therefore questioning the conventional practices of bodybuilding preparation."

Natural bodybuilding competition preparation and recovery: a 12-month case study (Rossow et al., 2013): "Heart rate decreased from 53- 27 beats/min during preparation and increased by 46 beats/min within 1 mo after competition. Brachial blood pressure dropped from 132/69 to 104/56 mmHg during preparation and returned to 116/64 mmHg at 6 mo after competition. Percent body fat declined from 14.8% to 4.5% during preparation and returned to 14.6% during recovery. Strength decreased during preparation and did not fully recover during 6 months of recovery. Testosterone declined from 9.22- 2.27 ng/mL during preparation and returned back to the baseline level, 9.91 ng/mL, after competition. Total mood disturbance increased from 6 to 43 units during preparation and recovered to 4 units 6 mo after competition."

[Diet and weight changes of female bodybuilders before and after competition (Walberg-Rankin et al., 1993)] "In details, the women followed stringent dietary control while getting ready for a competition but as the competition is over she followed a diet pattern of higher energy and fat consumption. These changes in diet and body weight may contribute to the instability until that time observed in the menstrual cycle of these athletes."

A pilot study was done by Ribeiro in the year 2015, on the male bodybuilders to find the effect of two verus three way split resistance training routines.

"The result was noticed that 4 and 6 weekly session frequencies of resistance training improve similar increases in fat free mass and muscular strength in prominent bodybuilders. Significant increases ($P < 0.05$) in fat-free mass (G4X = +4.2%, G6X = +3.5%) and muscular strength (G4X = +8.4%, G6X = +11.4%) with no group by time interaction were observed."

In 2013, Hackett conducted study on the male bodybuilders on the training practices and ergogenic aids.

"The conclusion of this study show that competitive bodybuilders act in accordance with present weight training exercise suggested for the compensation effect to muscle. During such process prior to competition through which the intensity and volume of resistance training will be reduced. This modification, if aerobic exercises volume is increased, is suggested to enhance the muscularity. But if the aerobic practice is continued there will be chances of losing the muscle mass in those natural compared with amateur bodybuilders who reportedly use drugs known to preserve muscle mass".

Contrasts in muscle and myo-fibers of elite male and female bodybuilders (Alway et al, 1989):

"Biceps CSA was positively correlated to fiber CSA (R = 0.75) and fiber number (R = 0.55). This recommended that by doing regular resistance training may be complicated and engaging fiber hypertrophy and fiber number (e.g., proliferation). Alternatively, since the muscle uniqueness prior to training is not known, this obvious variation might be genetically resolute feature."

Single Muscle Fibre Contractile Properties Differ Between Body-Builders, Power Athletes and Control Subjects (Meijer et al., 2015):

"Fiber cross-sectional area was 67 and 88% (P < 0.01) larger in BBs than in PAs and Cs, respectively, with no major difference in fiber cross-sectional area between PAs and Cs. Fibers of BBs and PAs developed a maximal isometric tension (32 and 50%, respectively, P < 0.01) than those of Cs. The specific tension of BB fibers was 62 and 41% lower than that of PA and C fibers (P < 0.05) respectively. Irrespective of fiber type, the peak power (PP) of PA fibers was 58% higher than that of BB fibers (P < 0.05), whereas BB fibers, despite considerable hypertrophy, had similar PP to the C fibers."

Skeletal muscle hypertrophy and structure and function of skeletal muscle fibers in male body builders (D'Antona et al., 2006)

"In BB a hypertrophy of fast and especially type 2X fiber was experimented. The very large hypertrophy of VL in vivo could not be fully accepted for by single muscle fibre hypertrophy. CSA of VL in vivo was, actuality 54% larger in BB than in CTRL whereas mean fibre area was only 14% larger in BB than in CTRL. MHC isoform distribution was shifted towards 2X fibres in BB. Po/CSA was significantly lower in type 1 fibres from BB than in type 1 fibres from CTRL whereas both type 2A and type 2X fibres were significantly stronger in BB than in CTRL. Vo of type 1 fibres and Vf of myosin 1 were significantly lower in BB than in CTRL, where no dissimilarity was noticed among fast fibres and myosin 2A. The result points out that skeletal muscle of BB was distinctly made to order to HHRE through extreme hypertrophy, a shift towards the bigger and more powerful fiber types and add to in definite force of muscle fibres.

The Misuse of Anabolic-Androgenic Steroids among Iranian Recreational Male Body-Builders and Their Related Psycho-Socio-Demographic factors (Angoorani and Halabchi, 2015): "Lifetime commonness of AAS mistreatment is comparatively elevated with recreational body-builders based on their self report. Some psycho-socio-demographic factors together with family income and sport experience may persuade the commonness of AAS abuse."

Body image disordered eating and anabolic steroid use in female bodybuilders (Goldfield, 2009):

"Competitive Bodybuilding is a sport the necessity of competitors will be lean and meso-morphic, so the competitors will be susceptible to the eating habits which are not healthy and controlling weight unethically, get addicted to anabolic steroids. It is observed that weight control and losing fat were given much priority, cut down many calories, bulimic practices and anabolic steroid use were information among CFBBs and to a lesser degree RFWTs. Dissimilarity between groups on common emotional factors were not fulfilling indications and outcome sizes were small. CFBBs contribute many eating connected features with women with bulimia nervosa but few emotional traits. Longitudinal research is required to find out whether women with eating habit problem or a history of bulimia nervosa unduly gravitate to competitive bodybuilding and/or whether competitive bodybuilding cultivates body dissatisfaction, disordered eating, bulimia nervosa, and anabolic steroid use."

Bodybuilders' body composition: effect of nandrolone decanoate (van Marken Lichtenbelt et al., 2004):

"The data shows that the direction of 200 mg.wk (-1) of ND (intramuscularly) for 8 wk enhance body mass and FFM whereas fat mass, bone mineral content, bone mineral density and the hydration of the FFM stay the same. This indicates that the enhancement can be related to an increase in muscle mass."

Body composition and anthropometry in bodybuilders: regional changes due to nandrolone decanoate administration (Hartgens et al., 2001):

The resultants of this paper state that, the intramuscular direction of nandrolone decanoate 200 mg/week for eight weeks will improve body weight and bone-free lean body mass in bodybuilders that show improvement in the trunk and legs known by DEXA.

Use of anabolic-androgenic steroids among body builders--frequency and attitudes (Lindstrom et al., 1990):

The study done on 138 male bodybuilders regularly doing weight training and the study was also to determined the effect of anabolic androgenic steroids and its adverse impact on vital organs, blood pressure, body mass index (BMI; kg m-2), training frequency, social background, occupation, knowledge and mind-set to steroid use. In 138 bodybuilders, for two years, 53 had used anabolic-androgenic steroids. The utilization of steroid was connected with higher BMI and more frequent training. The other 75 per cent (n = 18) of those attending body building for competition and 24% (n = 11) of those to increases their fitness, using anabolic-androgenic steroids. Of all body builders, 94% declared that anabolic-androgenic steroids are dangerous. Of the users, 81% faced side-effects, but 74% were still interested to continue steroid medication."

Increases in ghrelin and decreases in leptin without altering adiponectin during extreme weight loss in male competitive bodybuilders (Mäestu et al., 2008):

In the end, ghrelin focus considerably was maximum, but is covered up in situation of inadequate energy accessibility that is accompanied by reducing the body mass in male subjects with initial low body fat.

Motivations for Anabolic Steroid use Among Bodybuilders (Wright et al., 2000):

Nowaday there is much utilization of steroids and eagerness to gain huge and define body posture. Many bodybuilders are not much worried about the adverse effect of steroids and most of the bodybuilders think that anabolic steroids are harmless and people who are unsuccessful in doing any achievement blame steroids as harmful and suggest others not to use it. Many of youngster are getting attracted and motivated to use steroids is they was to excel in competition and want to get more define and massive, it is also known that steroids develop emotionally by boosting the confidence feeling. The really is that upcoming bodybuilders use loads of sample which are high level steroids and dangerous. Through study it is understood that awareness regarding the side effect of steroid must be motivated and circulated.

Nutrient intake, body fat, and lipid profiles of competitive male and female bodybuilders (Bazzarre et al., 1990)

This information is exclusive for the reason that the dimensions were known at the competition. Information is recorded for means and standard deviations. Estimated body fat for males (6.0 +/- 1.8%) and females (9.8 +/- 1.5%) was very low.

Supplementation patterns of competitive male and female bodybuilders (Brill and Keane 1994): This study explains the influence of supplement used on 309 male and female competitive bodybuilders. During the training phase variation of supplement were done. Fat cutter and amino acids were used to burn fat and Protein powder were used to bulk. Of bodybuilder 59 % percent of respondents spent $25-100 per month; 4.9% spent over $150. The main objective of using supplement was to achieve strength for heavy training. During bulking phase, anabolic supplement and weight gain were consumed frequently by men than women. In the cutting phase, fat burners were consumed by a greater percentage of females than males. The study can help sport nutritionists to guide bodybuilders towards more healthful nutrition practices.

Metabolic responses to high protein diet in Korean elite bodybuilders with high-intensity resistance exercise (Kim et al., 2011):

The diet in which large amounts of protein (4.3 ± 1.2 g/kg BW/day) and calories (5,621.7 ± 1,354.7 kcal/day) and intake of vitamins and minerals more than advice like potassium and calcium. Serum creatine (1.3 ± 0.1 mg/dl) and potassium (5.9 ± 0.8 mmol/L) and urinary urea nitrogen (24.7 ± 9.5 mg/dl) and creatine (2.3 ± 0.7 mg/dl) were noticed to be more than the range normal. Urinary calcium (0.3 ± 0.1 mg/dl) and phosphorus (1.3 ± 0.4 mg/dl) were just within the border and the urine pH was normal in range. In diet protein is high so there will be excretion of urea nitrogen and creatine is high due to which there will be increased urinary. It is clear that in this study the metabolic acidosis reaction to high protein diet in sample with intake of high potassium and vigorous weight training. This study provides explanation on the weight training with accurate amount of mineral supplementation like potassium and calcium could lower the side effects of protein-generated metabolic changes.

Summary of the Literature

From the review of related literature it was observed that there was immense scope for further research on influence of diet and weight training on HDL and LDL levels on endomorph bodybuilders on the basis of the experienced gained the investigator the possible method to be utilized for this research, that is presented in chapter 3.

CHAPTER III

METHODOLOGY

In this chapter, the process of selecting the subjects, collection of variables, reliability of methods, competency of suggestion taken from resourceful persons and research design and statistical procedure applied has been explained.

Procedure for selection and reliability of subjects:

Taking into consideration about the characteristic of endomorphs body types bodybuilders, such body types were monitored at the National competitions of Satish Jarkeholi competition and competitions conducted by (IBBF) Indian Bodybuilder's Federation. The bodybuilders were selected on the basis of endomorphs characteristics and were selected as research samples. This procedure of selecting the samples was carried out in the National competition since the year 2017 at the Satish Jarkeholi bodybuilding competition held at Belagavi. After the competition, the selected subjects were called to discuss about the research work with the cooperation of (BDBBA) Belgaum District Bodybuilders Association and few competition judges like Sunil N Aptekar, Ajit Siddannavar, Ranjit Killekar and Prakesh Pujari. The subjects agreed to provide their cooperation to follow the diet pattern and weight training pattern which was suggested by me to them during their next preparation for National competition that was going to be held in the month of March 2018 at Pune. This was possible with the help of Mr. Sunil N Aptekar, Ekalavya Awardee and Indian Coach for Bodybuilder's team and Ranjit Killekar, International Bodybuilder. Under the conceptive obtained from Mr. Sunil N Aptekar in the formal discussion on this topic, he agreed to the prepositions that were mentioned in the research study. It emphasized on aspects like why most of Indian bodybuilders were not able to make any achievement in the International competition, how such research study will help future bodybuilders to develop good quality muscles without using anabolic substance or any performance enhancing drugs, etc. Such studies on bodybuilders are taken up in few foreign universities by using electronic gadgets (like Electronic Stimulators, Transcutaneous Electric Nerve Stimulators, etc), by considering diet and supplementary control, etc, so they could use the appropriate training load to pump their muscles and to promote muscles mass in them. Such high tech equipments are very rarely seen in India and also such research study are usually overlooked or given less importance. Most of the study is done on the superficial level when it comes to bodybuilding, such as the effects of diet on bodybuilders or influence of weight training on muscles mass of bodybuilders. These studies will definitely help in designing weight training patterns or diet patterns but as the muscle structure and its effect varies from individual to individual, diet and weight training patterns of one kind cannot be implemented. There are many cases wherein a lot of bodybuilders are dying because of cardiac arrest (heart attack) and most of them think that it is usually due to the over usage of steroids but there could be many other reasons.

Further discussions were done with Mr. Sunil N Aptekar to discover different ways through which young bodybuilders can safely develop their muscles.

When the purpose of research was conveyed to him, he himself initiated to provide his assistance in the research right from selecting subjects and making them follow the direction given regarding diet and weight training pattern which were designed for them from the research point of view. The only problem that was faced during the discussion with the bodybuilders, was that most of the bodybuilders had a doubt of doping test and were in dilemma weather to give their blood samples for the research or not. In order to overcome this problem there was a decision taken altogether that anonymous collection of blood samples will be done. Later it was decided since January 2018 to March 2018, that diet and weight training will be followed under observation before the National competition and from March 2018 to June 2018 off season diet and weight training practices will be followed only as per the direction given to them. The blood samples were decided to be collected before five days of National competition and off season blood samples were to be collected in the month of June 2018. Discussions were also done with Mr. Ajit Siddanavar (Inter-National Judge and Secretary of Karnataka State Bodybuilders Association) who expressed extreme enthusiasm about the research study on bodybuilders as he had never come across such research study in India. He also instructed few bodybuilders to cooperate in the research study. After taking into consideration the request of the bodybuilders and giving them the consent about their names being kept anonymous, fifteen bodybuilders were selected for subjects group. The next task was the selection of gyms and convincing the gym proprietors and instructors to provide the relevant information about their gym clients which was necessary for the purpose of research study. Various gyms in the city were selected like Killerkar's Gym, Lokmanya Gym, Morya Gym, Corporation gym, Manikbag gym, Body tone gym and Body fitness gym to get access of the resources of gyms that were required for of a number of research works. With their further consent, permission was granted to select subjects and to monitor their training. While selecting subjects for the control group precaution were taken that the selected subjects are endomorphs body type and are regular to gym. The next stage was designing the diet pattern and weight training pattern for selected bodybuilders of subject groups and monitoring the regularity of control group.

Sufficient information was gathered on weight training workouts by visiting various gyms to observe the prominent workout design for weight training pattern. Taking the national bodybuilders into consideration the weight training pattern was designed for them. While designing the weight training pattern, guidance was taken from Mr. Sunil N Aptekar as all the selected bodybuilders of subject group where under his control. He was only to be informed about the pattern of diet and the direction about the weight training, as he further mediated the same to all the bodybuilders. On the contrary, the bodybuilders were personally monitored by visiting their gyms in their respective workout hours. A few of them were personally trained too. Simultaneously samples of control group were also monitored for weight training. The control group was only guided in case if they were performing wrong exercises or else they were not disturbed if regularity to the gym was maintained by them following their regular exercises routine.

Further, a diet pattern was decided to give carbohydrate 60%, protein 30% and fat 10%. This ratio remains almost same in most of the bodybuilder's diet. There were many other diet patterns but this diet pattern is traditionally considered ideal as the most of bodybuilders follow the same pattern. The guidance of Sunil N Aptekar and Dinesh Vernekar (Sports Nutritionist and certified K11Master coach), was seeked who adviced the same diet proportion. Assistance was taken from Dinesh Vernekar to design diet pattern for competition season as well as off season for National bodybuilders. The calories for competition were minimum compared to the calorie of off season. In the diet pattern intake of food supplement is also included.

The samples were monitored from the months of January 2018 to March 2018 for competition season and after completing National competition that was to be held on 28th March onwards till the end of June 2018 for offseason. Bodybuilder's blood samples were collected five days before they go for National competition as collection of fasting blood samples of fifteen bodybuilders was not possible in one day. So on, selected dates were given to every bodybuilder and were instructed to be on time at the selected gyms to give blood samples. The same instructions were provided to control group as well.

Further after national competition, bodybuilders were provided with off season workout pattern and diet pattern which was to be followed till the end of the June 2018. In the end of June 2018, blood samples were collected all over again as per the collection procedure mentioned during the collection of blood sample at National competition.

After collection of blood samples, the samples were sent to Sidhi Hi-tech labortory to analyse the data for HDL and LDL.

Selection of Subjects:

Thirty endomorph body type body builders of age group belonging to 20-30 years and weighing above 75 kgs who are participating in the National Level Bodybuilding competitions will be selected as subjects for research study.

The above thirty endomorph body builders (subjects) will be divided into the following two categories:-

1) 15 endomorphs national bodybuilders of whose HDL & LDL will be studied- known as Subject group
2) 15 normal weight trainers who are endomorphs and doing gym workout daily- known as Control group.
3) Subject group diet and weight training pattern will be monitored for 3 months before competition (January to March, 2018) and 3 months in off season (March to June, 2018).
4) Control group will be guided for proper weight training and normal daily diet which is required to maintain their fitness.

5) Care was taken that the selected subjects had no genetic cholesterol history.

6) Gym Clients with Endomorphs body type were selected for Control Group.

7) Subject group's diet and weight training pattern were monitored since Feb 2018.

The above said procedure will be followed after the selection of national bodybuilders of endomorphs body types.

Selection of Variables:

The researcher revived the various scientific literatures pertaining to body types, High density lipoproteins and low density lipoproteins, weight training methods, diet patterns from books and web addresses etc and taking into consideration, the feasibility and availability of methods the following variables were selected.

Criterion variable

- Endomorph bodybuilders
- HDL and LDL profile

Determinant Variables

The following variables were selected as identification of endomorph body type.

Details of Endomorph body type:

Lean muscle, round face, small neck, heavy fat storage, broad hip, large structure, Photos of prior to bodybuilding were used to identify body types of the subjects before selecting them for the research work.

Endomorphs body type is: Soft musculature, thick rib cage, Short neck, Heavy fat storage, wide hips, mostly over weight/obese and huge structure. Endo-morphs with characteristic of great fat cell and slower metabolism rate turn ingested food into stored body fat. They have to eat enough protein, but otherwise have to keep their caloric intake to a minimum. This means making sure that no more than 20% of their calories come in the form of fat. But about 20% of endomorphs lower-than-average thyroid output which compounds the problems. However, although they always have to work harder at keeping lean, they tend to built muscles relatively easily compared to ectomorph, and they can eventually lose a lot of excess body fat by diet and exercises.

About HDL and LDL cholesterol in detail:

Meaning and details of HDL cholesterol- HDL refers to High Density Lipoprotein Cholesterol. It is cholesterol is said to be harmless cholesterol and it is considered to be a friendly lipoprotein which travels through the blood stream. The chief objective is to remove harmful cholesterol which will be in the damaged region of the arteries in the form of plaque from where it is not belong. There will be low risk of heart disease if the level of HDL is high and low HDL levels increases the chances of cardiac problems. HDL in body is increases by our daily life style like by doing regular exercises, maintaining ideal body weight and not getting addicted to bad habits.

The normal human level of HDL cholesterol will be 30 to 75 mg/ dl. If the HDL level of cholesterol is 60 mg/ dl or higher it prevent heart diseases.

Meaning and details of LDL: LDL cholesterol refers to Low Density Lipoprotein cholesterol, is said to harmful cholesterol. If the level of LDL is above the normal range then there are high chances of heart related diseases. The lipids are the formation of lipoprotien which are fusion of fat or lipids and protein which flow in our blood. The average man has an LDL cholesterol level of 60 to 160 mg/ dl. An LDL cholesterol level which is less than 100mg/ dl is considered to be ideal.

(The present research study aims to find the levels of HDL and LDL which could be useful in development of muscles in body builders because of weight training, maintaining of diet and utilization of food supplements. Here the data obtained from the blood sample reports of body builders is collected basically measuring their HDL and LDL levels during the competition phase and off competition phase. Further, the body builders taken under study are classified into subject and control group.

Reliability of Data

The reliability of data was ensured through scientific methods the investigator was satisfied with the outcome of the results.

Laboratory method to detect HDL and LDL:

Muscle development difference between HDL and LDL of body builders will be measured by taking biochemical test (laboratory method) during off season and competition season. Diet pattern and weight training methods will be noted for off season and competition season.

Subjects and control groups 4ml fasting blood samples were collected in the month of March before National level competition and in the month of June after completing off Season. Further, the samples will be analyzed for HDL and LDL at the Laboratory.

Procedure of collecting and analyzing the blood samples to identify the levels of HDL and LDL:

Clinical Significance of Low Density Lipoprotein (LDL):

It is known that if the LDL range is increased in the body there is risk of coronary heart disease and is related with overweight, obesity, diabetes and nephritis. This occurs when the plaque is formed in the arteries and this happens because of LDL particles so it is considered as harmful or bad cholesterol.

Clinical Diagnosis should not make on a single test result, it should integrate clinical and other laboratory data.

Clinical Significance of High Density Lipo-protein (HDL):

It is known that if the harmless or good or friendly cholesterol because the increased range of HDL particles carry lipo-protiens into the blood which helps to remove the plaques formation in the arteries which later create blockage in the natural blood flow resulting in high chances of coronary artery and cardiac problems.

Clinical diagnosis should not be made on a single test result it should integrate clinical and other laboratory data.

Method used on blood samples:

Direct Enzymatic Calorimetric Method was used on blood samples to detect the levels of HDL and LDL.

Normal Range:

1) HDL – 30 to 75 mg/dl
2) LDL - 60 to 160 mg/dl

For HDL,

Principle:- The assay consists of the separate response test:-

1) Removal of Chylomicron (CM), LDL cholesterol and VLDL- cholesterol by cholesterol esterase, cholesterol oxidize and catalyses in reagent 1 this is colorless reaction.
2) Specific reaction of HDL-cholesterol after release of HDL-C by detergent in Reagent 2.

For LDL,

Principle: The assay consists of distinct reaction steps:-

1) The LDL complex with poly-anion. The detergent 1 in reagent 1 is soluble only in the non-LDL lipoprotein particles the cholesterol released will be used up by enzymatic reagent and be in a non-color forming reaction without the Chromogenic coupler.
2) The cholesterol released from LDL-C by detergent 2 in reagent 2 reacts with Chromogenic coupler for the color formation.

Table: 3.1 showing the explanation of the reagents used during the anaylsis of the blood sample for HDL and LDL test

HDL reagent contains	LDL reagent contains
R1 – Cholesterol esterase >/- 1000 U/L	R1 – Poly-anion
- Cholesterol Oxidase >/- 800 U/L	- Detergent 1 - 0.5% - Cholesterol esterase >/- 800 U/L

- Catalyst	>/-	900 U/L	- Cholesterol Oxidase	>/-	400 U/L
- TOOS	>/-	100 U/L	- Peroxides	>/-	5000 U/L
R2 – 4- aminoantipyrine			- 4- aminoantipyrine	-	100 mmol/L
- Detergent	-	0.5%	- TOSS		
- Peroxidase	-	>/- 4000 U/L	R2 – Detergent 2	-	2%
- Sodium azide	-	100 mmol/L	- TOSS	-	100 mmol/L
HDL$_{c/}$ Calibrator – Lyophilized human serum			LDL$_{c/}$ Calibrator – lyophilized human serum		

Sample Collection :- (Specimen)

- Early morning fasting blood samples should be collected to get the accurate result.
- No sample should be collected after meals. Because the food contains lipoproteins in it and it may varies the result in blood.
- It should be collected in the plan starile vacutainer with no any anticoagulant like citrate should not be use after it gets clot.
- Serum or heparinized plasma gets separated and it should be free of hemolysis.
- (Sample should be centrifuge and their serum should be separated) serum sample will be ready for testing.

Materials required for the test:

1) Spectrophotometer or calorimeter measuring at 6:00 am.
2) Metched cuvettes 1.0 cm light path.
3) General laboratory equipments like
- Glass test tubes
- Tissues papers to clean tubes
- Advanced micro calibrated pippet
- Distilled water/ normal saline to clean the mashine.
- Patients sample (Blood Serum)

- Plastic disposable micro pippets tips
- Printer to print the result
- Reagent kit from the various companies like (ERBA, Euro, Sprinchat etc)
- Quality control sample which is provided by the companies.
- 1% sodium hypochloride solution in a flask to dispose or discard use micro tips.

Machine used:

ERBA CHEM 5 plus V2 Biochemistry Analyzers

Procedure:

1) Adjust the machine wavelength - 600-700 nm
2) Cuvette   - 1cm light path
3) Temperature   - 37^{0}C.
4) Adjust the instrument to zero with distilled water
5) Take the three test tubes and pipette out into.

Regent (ml)	Blank (ml)	Calibrator (ml)	Sample (ml)
Sample	-	-	(10 ml)
Calibrator (ml)	-	(10 ml)	-
Water (ml)	(10 ml)	-	-
R1 (ml)	(450 ml)	(450 ml)	(450 ml)

6) Mix all the test tubes and incubate at 37 ^{0}C for 5 min's.
7) And the add reagent 2 (R2)

Regent	Blank	Calibrator	Sample
R2 (ml)	150 ml	150 ml	150 ml

8) Mix all the test tubes and incubate at 37^{0}C for 5 min's.
9) Now regulate the absorbance of the blank to zero
10) Now take the reading producing each test tube to the machine absorbance
11) Record the result and calculate by following formula.

Calculation: - For LDL

Mg/dl LDL_C in sample = A calibrator/ A sample X Concentrated of calibrator

This formula is used for automated machines

Conversion factors:- mg/dl X 0.02586 = mmol/L

mmol/L X 38.67 = mg/dl

Result: …………………. mg/dl.

*Procedure is same for both HDL and LDL.

General instruction:

- The fasting blood samples (4ml) of both the subject and control group, in the month of March, before the subjects go for their national competition and in February, after completion of their off season duration.
- The collected fasting blood samples of both the seasons were analyzed at Siddhi Clinical Laboratory, Belagavi .

After getting the results from the laboratory of subject and control group, the data is given to statistical analyst for the comparison of data.

The comparison of HDL and LDL measures (during the competition phase and off competition phase) is done for the subject and control group using the independent t-test for comparison of two means (t-test is used as it's a comparison between two groups and the sample size may be less than 30)

Weight Training Pattern - The training method selected for subject group is compound exercise with super sets. The weight training load recommended for the competition group is progressive weight load.

Table no 3.2 showing the weight training pattern given to the subject group during competition and off season.

Timing for gym: morning 7.00 to 9.00 am and evening 6.30 to 8.30 pm.

a) After 30 min's warming up workout

- Monday & Thursday (Chest & back exercise)
- Tuesday & Friday (Shoulder & Arms exercise)
- Wednesday & Saturday (Thighs & Calf exercise)

- Abdominal exercise will be of 4 sets for each muscle.
- Main frame workout will be of 4 sets of 20,18,16,14 or 12 repetitions with moderate weights.

  b) In off competition: 30 min's warming workout and main frame workout of same pattern but with reduced repetitions of 14,12,10,8 or 6 reps and heavy weights. Abdominal exercise will be of 3 sets each muscle

  Monday & Thursday (Chest & back exercise), Tuesday & Friday (Shoulder & Arms exercise), Wednesday & Saturday (Thighs & Calf exercise), Abdominal exercise will be of 4 sets for each muscle (Upper, lower and oblique).

- Main frame workout will be of 5 sets of 20,18,16,14 & 12 repetitions with moderate weights.
- In off competition: 30 min's warming workout and main frame workout of same pattern but with reduced repetitions of 14,12,10,8 & 6 reps and heavy weights.
- Abdomen, forearms, claves exercises on daily routine.

Chest Exercises:

1) Bench press (Barbell or Dumbbell) 2) Dumbbell Fly 3) Incline Press (Barbell or Dumbbell) 4) Incline dumbbell fly, 5) Decline press (Barbell or Dumbbell) 6) Cross Cable (optional)

Back Exercises:

1) Lat Machine pulley 2) Medium grip pulley (optional) 3) T-Bar rowing 4) Barbell Rowing (optional) 5) one arm dumbbell/barbell/cable rowing 6) seated cable rowing (Ground Pulley) 7) Dead lifts

Shoulder Exercises:

1) Barbell/Dumbbell Press 2) Behind Neck Barbell Press (optional) 3) Standing/seating Lateral Dumbbell/Cable/Barbell raise 4) Arnold Press 5) upright rowing 6) Dumbbell/barbell Shrugs 6) Front Dumbbell raises.

Arms Exercises:

A) Biceps

1) Alternate Dumbbell curls 2) Arm Blaster Curls (optional) 3) Preacher Curls 4) Incline dumbbell curls 5) Hammer curls 6) Concentration Curls.

B) Triceps

1) Cable Press down 2) one-arm cable reverse press downs 3) Seating/Standing Triceps press with Dumbbell/Barbell 4) Lying extension with dumbbell/Barbell 5) Standing/ Lying cross face cable extension (optional) 6) Close grip barbell press for triceps.

Thighs Exercises:

1) Dumbbell/Barbell Squats 2) Half Squats (optional) 3) Front Squats 4) Sissy Sit ups (optional) 5) Leg Press 6) Hack Squats (optional) 7) Leg extension & Curls 8) Straight Leg Dead lifts (optional)

Claves

1) Standing Calf raises 2) Leg press calf raises 3) seated calf raises 4) Donkey/load calf raises 5) Reverse calf raises

Abdomen

1) Bend Leg Crunches 2) Vertical Bench Crunches 3) twisting crunches 4) Leg raises 5) Side leg raises 6) Bench Kick backs (optional) 7) Vacuum

Diet Chart:

- Protein 60%, carbohydrate 30% & fat 10 % of 2069 calories, during competition season for subject group.
- Carbohydrate 60%, protein 30% & fat 10 % of 3269 calories, during off season will be monitored for subject group.
- Control group will be on daily routine food.

Table no 3.3 showing the diet chart given to the subject group during competition.

Competition Diet:

Time	Meals
5.30 – 6.00 am	1 scoop whey in water Supplements: 1 tablet B-complex
9.30 – 10.00 am	6 egg whites 3 chapatti with any green leafy bhaji Supplements: 1 tablet Calcium
12.30 – 1.30 pm	125 gm cooked in 2 tbsp oil chicken/fish/paneer 100 gm brown rice with dal 1 big bowl of green leafy sabzi 200 gm dahi Supplements: 1 tablet omega 3
5.00 – 6.00 pm	Tea/coffee add sugarfree 6 egg whites and 1 whole egg 2 brown bread
9.00 – 9.30 pm	125 gm boiled chicken/fish/paneer 100 gm brown rice with dal 1 big bowl of green leafy sabzi 200 gm dahi Supplements: 2 tablets Limcee 1 tablets Evion 400 mg 1 tablet omega 3

Table no 3.4 showing the calorie consumption by the subject ground during the during competition season.

Calorie chart of competition diet plan:

	Protein	Fat	Carbohydrate	Calories
Meals 1	20	2	2	106
Meals 2	28	5	50	357
Meals 3	45	8	100	652
Meals 4	24	5	40	301
Meals 5	45	8	100	653
	162	28	292	2069

Table no 3.5 showing the calorie consumption by the subject during offseason season.

Calorie chart of offseason plan:

	Protein	Fat	Carbohydrate	Calories
Meals 1	26	2	40	282
Meals 2	38	10	120	722
Meals 3	70	10	150	970
Meals 4	30	5	40	325
Meals 5	70	10	150	970
	236	37	500	3269

Table no 3.6 showing the diet chart given to the subject group during offseason.

Off season diet:

Time	Meals
5.30 – 6.00 am	1 scoop whey in water Add 40 gms oats Supplements: 1 tablet B-complex
9.30 – 10.00 am	8 egg whites 5 chapatti with any green leafy bhaji Supplements: 1 tablet Calcium
12.30 – 1.30 pm	200 gm cooked in 2 tbsp oil chicken/fish/paneer 150 gm brown rice with dal 1 big bowl of green leafy sabzi 200 gm dahi Supplements: 1 tablet omega 3
5.00 – 6.00 pm	Tea/coffee add sugarfree 6 egg whites and 1 whole egg 4 brown bread
9.00 – 9.30 pm	200 gm boiled chicken/fish/paneer 150 gm brown rice with dal 1 big bowl of green leafy sabzi 200 gm dahi Supplements: 2 tablets Limcee 1 tablets Evion 400 mg 1 tablet omega 3

RESEARCH DESIGN

This research aims to find out the levels of HDL and LDL which could be useful in development of muscles in body builders because of weight training, maintaining of diet and utilization of food supplement.

STATISTICAL ANALYSIS

The sample data is analyzed using t-test for independent sample, as it is comparison between two independent groups i.e. subject group and control group.

- **t-test for comparison of two means**
  Blood sample reports were obtained from subject group and control group (during the competition phase and off competition phase) in terms of their HDL and LDL levels.

  Here the average measure of HDL/LDL level of Subject Group was compared with the average measure of HDL/LDL level of Control Group during the competition phase as well as off competition phase. Here the number of experimental units will be of thirty. The correct tool to analyze the data for the comparison of two means is "t-test".

- **About t-test**
  In the given research study it is hypothesis that the level of significance is to be fixed at 5%. The SPSS software (Statistical Package for Social Science) was used to carry out t-test, this t-test is appropriate whenever the sample size is less than or equal to 30 units and if the sample size exceeds above 30 units then the software automatically generate resulted from small sample test (t-test) to large sample test (Z-test).

  Here we are using t-test for two means (independent samples) since we are comparing the average measure of HDL and LDL levels of Subject Group with average measure of HDL and LDL levels of Control Group.

  To carry out the t-test for comparison of two means, we first carry out Levene's test for equality of variances. If the p-value (significant value) under Levene's test for equality of variances is not more than the level of significance (5% i.e. 0.05) then we observe the p-value (significant value) for the t-test with equal variances not assumed else we observe the p-value for the t-test with equal variances assumed.

Further if the p-value under the t-test is less than the level of significance (5% i.e. 0.05) than the null hypothesis is rejected else it would be accepted at the given level of significance.

1) Analyzation of data done by biochemical test for Lipoproteins will be used for statistical tool.

2) As the number of experimental units is 30, t-test is used for comparison of two means as it was the appropriate tool for analyzing the data.

CHAPTER IV

ANALYSIS OF DATA AND RESULTS OF THE STUDY

Descriptive Statistic about the sample units under this study

Lowest age: 20 years

Highest age: 30 years

Sample Unit: 30 sizes

Age Distribution of the sample Unit

Age Group	Total	Percentage
20-22	02	6.66 %
23-25	10	33.33 %
26-28	08	26.66 %
29-31	10	33.33 %
Sample unit =	30	

Out of the total sample of the National level bodybuilders are investigated, maximum numbers of unit/participants are belonging to the age groups are 23-25 and 29-31 (33-33%) and the minimum numbers of unit/participants belonging to the age group is 20-22 (6.66%).

Data Analysis

H_{N1}: There is no significant difference between the Subject and Control Group with respect to HDL readings during Competition Phase.

H_{A1}: There is a significant difference between the Subject and Control Group with respect to HDL readings during Competition Phase.

Table no 4.1 showing the Mean, Standard Deviation values for HDL reading on subjects and control groups during competition phase.

Group Statistics

	Group Category of the Respondent	N	Mean	Std. Deviation	Std. Error Mean
HDL Reading (mg/dl) during Competion Phase (March)	Subject Group	15	39.73	6.053	1.563
	Control Group	15	41.33	2.895	.747

Table no 4.2 Levene's test for equality of Variances for HDL reading during competition phase.

Independent Samples Test

		Levene's Test for Equality of Variances		t-test for Equality of Means						95% Confidence Interval of the Difference	
		F	Sig.	t	df	Sig. (2-tailed)	Mean Difference	Std. Error Difference		Lower	Upper
HDL Reading (mg/dl) during Competion Phase (March)	Equal variances assumed	10.594	.003	-.924	28	.364	-1.600	1.732		-5.149	1.949
	Equal variances not assumed			-.924	20.087	.367	-1.600	1.732		-5.213	2.013

Inference: The above hypothesis is tested at 5% (0.05) level of significance. From the Levene's Test we observe that the p-value (0.003) is less than 5% (0.05) level of significance. Hence we have to carry out the t-test with equal variances not assumed. Here in the t-test we observe that the p-value (0.367) is greater than the level of significance (0.05), hence we cannot reject the null hypothesis (H_{N1}) at 5% level of significance.

Conclusion: There is no significant difference between the Subject and Control Group with respect to HDL readings during the Competition Phase at 5% (0.05) level of significance.

Interpretation: There is no significant difference of influence of diet and weight training on the Subject and Control groups of endomorph bodybuilders with respect to HDL levels during competition season phase.

H_{N2} : There is no significant difference between the Subject and Control Group with respect to LDL readings during the Competition Phase.

H_{A2} : There is significant difference between the Subject and Control Group with respect to LDL readings during the Competition Phase.

Table no 4.3 showing the Mean, Standard Deviation values for LDL reading on subjects and control groups during competition phase.

Group Statistics

	Group Category of the Respondent	N	Mean	Std. Deviation	Std. Error Mean
LDL Reading (mg/dl) during Competion Phase (March)	Subject Group	15	98.93	14.479	3.738
	Control Group	15	85.33	5.233	1.351

Table no 4.4 Levene's test for equality of Variances for LDL reading during competition phase.

Independent Samples Test

		Levene's Test for Equality of Variances		t-test for Equality of Means						95% Confidence Interval of the Difference	
		F	Sig.	t	df	Sig. (2-tailed)	Mean Difference	Std. Error Difference	Lower	Upper
LDL Reading (mg/dl) during Competion Phase (March)	Equal variances assumed	7.569	.010	3.421	28	.002	13.600	3.975	5.457	21.743
	Equal variances not assumed			3.421	17.596	.003	13.600	3.975	5.235	21.965

Inference: The above hypothesis is tested at 5% (0.05) level of significance. From the Levene's Test we observe that the p-value (0.010) is less than 5% (0.05) level of significance. Hence we have to carry out the t-test with equal variances not assumed. Here in the t-test we observe that the p-value (0.003) is less than the level of significance (0.05), hence we can reject the null hypothesis (H_{N2}) at 5% level of significance.

Conclusion: There is a significant difference between the Subject and Control Group with respect to LDL readings during Competition Phase at 5% (0.05) level of significance. *From the table of descriptive statistics, we see that Average LDL reading in Subject Group (98.93) is greater as compared to the Control Group (85.33)*

Interpretation: There is significant difference of influence of diet and weight training on the Subject and Control groups of endomorph bodybuilders with respect to LDL levels during competition season phase. Hence this shows even though LDL is bad cholesterol it helps in development of muscles during competition phase.

H_{N3}: There is no significant difference between the Subject and Control Group with respect to HDL readings during Off-Season Phase.

H_{A3}: There is a significant difference between the Subject and Control Group with respect to HDL readings during Off-Season Phase.

Table 4.5 showing the Mean, Standard Deviation values for HDL reading on subjects and control groups during offseason phase.

Group Statistics

	Group Category of the Respondent	N	Mean	Std. Deviation	Std. Error Mean
HDL Reading (mg/dl) during Off-Season Phase (June)	Subject Group	15	47.40	5.110	1.319
	Control Group	15	42.40	3.112	.804

Table no 4.6 Levene's test for equality of Variances for HDL reading during offseason phase.

Independent Samples Test

		Levene's Test for Equality of Variances		t-test for Equality of Means						
									95% Confidence Interval of the Difference	
		F	Sig.	t	df	Sig. (2-tailed)	Mean Difference	Std. Error Difference	Lower	Upper
HDL Reading (mg/dl) during Off-Season Phase (June)	Equal variances assumed	3.145	.087	3.236	28	.003	5.000	1.545	1.835	8.165
	Equal variances not assumed			3.236	23.129	.004	5.000	1.545	1.805	8.195

Inference: The above hypothesis is tested at 5% (0.05) level of significance. From the Levene's Test we observe that the p-value (0.087) is greater than 5% (0.05) level of significance. Hence we have to carry out the t-test with equal variances assumed. Here in the t-test we observe that the p-value (0.003) is less than the level of significance (0.05), hence we can reject the null hypothesis (H_{N3}) at 5% level of significance.

Conclusion: There is a significant difference between the Subject and Control Group with respect to HDL readings during Off-Season Phase at 5% (0.05) level of significance. *From the table of descriptive statistics, we see that Average HDL reading in Subject Group (47.40) is greater as compared to the Control Group (42.40)*

Interpretation: There is significant difference of influence of diet and weight training on the Subject and Control groups of endomorph bodybuilders with respect to HDL levels during offseason phase and Hence this show though HDL is more in subject group then control group during off season.

H_{N4}: There is no significant difference between the Subject and Control Group with respect to LDL readings during Off-Season Phase.

H_{A4}: There is a significant difference between the Subject and Control Group with respect to LDL readings during Off-Season Phase.

Table no 4.7 showing the Mean, Standard Deviation values for LDL reading on subjects and control groups during off-season phase.

Group Statistics

	Group Category of the Respondent	N	Mean	Std. Deviation	Std. Error Mean
LDL Reading (mg/dl) during Off-Season Phase (June)	Subject Group	15	90.87	12.766	3.296
	Control Group	15	85.00	6.698	1.729

Table 4.8 Levene's test for equality of Variances for LDL reading during offseason phase.

Independent Samples Test

		Levene's Test for Equality of Variances		t-test for Equality of Means						95% Confidence Interval of the Difference	
		F	Sig.	t	df	Sig. (2-tailed)	Mean Difference	Std. Error Difference		Lower	Upper
LDL Reading (mg/dl) during Off-Season Phase (June)	Equal variances assumed	3.928	.057	1.576	28	.126	5.867	3.722		-1.758	13.492
	Equal variances not assumed			1.576	21.164	.130	5.867	3.722		-1.871	13.604

Inference: The above hypothesis is tested at 5% (0.05) level of significance. From the Levene's Test we observe that the p-value (0.057) is greater than 5% (0.05) level of significance. Hence we have to carry out the t-test with equal variances assumed. Here in the t-test we observe that the p-value (0.126) is greater than the level of significance (0.05), hence we cannot reject the null hypothesis (H_{N4}) at 5% level of significance.

Conclusion:

There is no significant difference between the Subject and Control Group with respect to LDL readings during Off-Season Phase at 5% (0.05) level of significance.

Interpretation: There is no significant difference of influence of diet and weight training on the Subject and Control groups of endomorph bodybuilders with respect to LDL levels during offseason phase.

Hence (H_{A2}) and (H_{A3}) hypothesis are positive according to the research. Whereas (H_{N1}), (H_{N4}) state that there is no significance in HDL and LDL during their phases.

According to the statistical analysis the outcome of the research state that the LDL during the competition phases is more than the HDL and so it is discovered that LDL is necessary for muscle development.

Discussion on Hypothesis:

It is also discovered through the statistical analysis that HDL level will be more in body during off season (non competition season) compare to LDL in bodybuilders and it is also discovered through the statistical analysis that HDL level will be more in body during off season (non competition season) compare to LDL in bodybuilders.

H_{N1}: There is no significant difference between the Subject and Control Group with respect to HDL readings during Competition Phase.

H_{A1}: There is a significant difference between the Subject and Control Group with respect to HDL readings during Competition Phase.

H_{N2}: There is no significant difference between the Subject and Control Group with respect to LDL readings during Competition Phase.

H_{A2}: There is a significant difference between the Subject and Control Group with respect to LDL readings during Competition Phase.

From the table of descriptive statistics, we see that Average LDL reading in Subject Group (98.93) is greater as compared to the Control Group (85.33)

H_{N3}: There is no significant difference between the Subject and Control Group with respect to HDL readings during Off-Season Phase.

H_{A3}: There is a significant difference between the Subject and Control Group with respect to HDL readings during Off-Season Phase.

From the table of descriptive statistics, we see that Average HDL reading in Subject Group (47.40) is greater as compared to the Control Group (42.40)

H_{N4}: There is no significant difference between the Subject and Control Group with respect to LDL readings during Off-Season Phase.

H_{A4}: There is a significant difference between the Subject and Control Group with respect to LDL readings during Off-Season Phase.

<h1 style="text-align:center">CHAPTER V</h1>

<h1 style="text-align:center">SUMMARY, CONCLUSIONS AND RECOMMENDATIONS</h1>

Summary:

Sports are a source through which one can attain an overall healthy life. It not only develops ones overall personality but also helps in attaining a disease free body. Our body is controlled by our mind, whereas, playing sports results in an ideal balance between our mind and our body. On the other hand, when it comes to making career in sports is a great option to be dealt with, provided it is done in a safer manner. After all our body is that thing in the world which is with us at every stage of our life. Each and every activity that we do to live our life, our body is directly involved with it. Thus taking care of the well being of our body is indeed a duty ought to be performed.

Bodybuilding is that form of physical activity that re-builds an individual's body in way far better than its original form, as each and every part of the body is trained differently with required specifications so that a desired muscle development is achieved. That is why bodybuilding is called as one such sport that defines one's body. It refers to a series of dedicated activities that result in body transformation. This not only means the outlook of the body at the outer level but the inner composition of the body also changes i.e. change in muscle fibers, muscle tissue, levels of lipoproteins, etc at a major level. All these changes when take place in a natural manner with extreme hard work and dedication, it makes wonders but when it is stimulated in an artificial manner for quick results it can turn to be harmful. The major effect of the weight training schedule and diets that are followed in the off season and competition season falls on the HDL and LDL levels of the body. This so happens because the fat in the diet is completely controlled in the competition season and then consumed in significant quantities in the off season. The same applies to weight training schedule which is rigorous in the competition season and a little lenient in the off season. These changes in the diet and weight training pattern bring about drastic variations in the HDL and LDL levels in the blood.

The purpose of this study was to determine what effects do the good and bad cholesterol have on the muscle development in a bodybuilder's body (specifically endomorphs body types) and which are the other influencing factors that could add on to the effect of the same. On the other hand the research also aimed to find out which is the cholesterol (HDL or LDL) that majorly affects the muscle mass and bodybuilding. To find out the same the investigator was in need to choose subjects that belonged to endomorph body type and who were national bodybuilders (for (experimental) subject group i.e. 15 in number) and weight trainers (for control group i.e. 15 in number) so as to attain full a fledged bodybuilder physique.

To proceed in the research, the investigator was in need to perform blood tests on the national bodybuilders that were endomorph body type in nature and thus the investigator choose 30 endomorph builders who could cooperate and agree for the blood tests. Therefore, before commencing the blood tests of the bodybuilders, it was conveyed and explained to the bodybuilders on how important this topic was and how greatly it could contribute to the field of body building and in the lives of the bodybuilders. Based on the explanation given to the subjects, immense cooperation was achieved from them. To proceed in the research it was necessary to take blood samples of the selected subjects in the duration prior and post competition so as to make investigations on the levels of HDL and LDL which are influenced due to the changes in diet and weight training patterns. To perform this blood test, 30 bodybuilders of endomorphs body type were chosen out of which 15 were (experimental) subject group and 15 were considered for control group.

The study has revealed how the levels of HDL and LDL affect the muscle building in the body of a Bodybuilder. And ways in which it could be prevented with the effective diet plans and exercise routine. It is been proved through this research that LDL is excess in the body during the completion phase and plays an important role in the development of muscle in the body of the bodybuilders. During the off season, HDL will be excessive in body that helps in the reduction of level of cholesterol in the body.

HYPOTHESIS

1. It is hypothesized that, finding the levels of HDL (High Density Lipoproteins) and LDL (Low Density Lipoproteins) are related in development of muscles in body builders.

2. It is hypothesized that, variation in lipoprotein (HDL and LDL) are responsible for the variations in muscles mass and helpful in development of muscles in bodybuilders.

3. To verify whether there exists a significant difference between the Subject and Control Group with respect to HDL readings during Competition Phase.

4. It is hypothesized that there is no significant difference between the Subject and Control Group with respect to LDL readings during Competition Phase.

5. It is hypothesized that there is no significant difference between the Subject and Control Group with respect to HDL readings during Off-Season Phase.

6. It is hypothesized that there is no significant difference between the Subject and Control Group with respect to LDL readings during Off-Season Phase.

Signification of the Study:

1) Through this research I would like to analyze the contribution of HDL and LDL in the development of muscles in endomorphs bodybuilders.
2) On base of LDL & HDL readings, the test can also be used by NADO, IOC, IPC and WADA for doping.
3) If HDL and LDL data is studied with insulin data, there is much scope for study related to overweight/obesity problems and maintenance of fitness.
4) This research may also explain why few bodybuilders died or dying because of cardiac arrest while performing on the stage during competition.
5) The study also serves to be useful in dealing with the aging phenomena related with muscles loss.
6) Study will also show why steroids are taken by bodybuilders.

CONCLUSION OF RESEARCH:

A common man also gets scared of the word "Cholesterol" it is often connected with serious health issues related with heart diseases. Well most of us know when the word cholesterol is referred to, we think of two aspects, one is "Good Cholesterol" and another one "Bad Cholesterol".

High Density Lipoproteins (HDL) is referred as Good Cholesterol and Low Density Lipoproteins are (LDL) is referred as Bad Cholesterol. But according to the research it is proved that Bad Cholesterol is not bad after all. The research data shows that you need some amount of LDL to be circulated in your blood to induce adequate muscle hypertrophy.

The research study states that after an intense exercise, bodybuilders who had developed most muscles mass also displayed the highest amount of LDL. Actually in the beginning of my study I had assumed that HDL will be necessary for muscles development as it is called as Good Cholesterol and at the end of my research, outcome was unexpected and surprising to me.

According to the research, it shows that both types of cholesterols are necessary for healthy condition of a human body. By thinking to remove bad cholesterol completely from our body if we get rid from diseases which are related with LDL then we are completely wrong. If we do that and remove LDL from our body we may not survive.

Low Density Lipoproteins (LDL) when it is traveling in blood, it gets stuck in the walls of arteries and such numbers of LDL get attached to the stack LDL (Plaque) which increases the LDL sizes, which give less space for blood to circulate in the arteries and if this condition further increases it may relate to heart diseases and heart attacks. The same condition can be in the artery in head and increases the risk of a stroke. Hence because of this mechanism LDL is named as Bad Cholesterol.

Whereas High Density Lipoproteins (HDL) it removes the stack cholesterol from the arteries and sends them to the liver for recycling. Because of this reason HDL is named as Good Cholesterol.

Presence of LDL is also a characteristic of understanding that there is something wrong and alerts the defense mechanism of body; hence it also serves as "warning sign".

The common thinking of everyone of getting rid of bad cholesterols is not a good understanding. They really need to educate themselves that both the cholesterols at certain range are necessary for body to lead a healthy life.

Cholesterol is important for our tissues and LDL provides it, where as cholesterol is cleaned up after when the repair is done and HDL is responsible for it. If the LDL is more in the blood (but within the normal range) is the better you are able to develop the muscles with weight training. This happens because LDL's main function is to transport the cholesterol to the tissues and tissues needs cholesterols to make hormones as well as to maintaining the cell membrane integrity. This explains why LDL will be more in National bodybuilders compare to HDL during the phase of competition.

- **Drugs that raise cholesterol levels in body**
  Beta Blockers, Estrogen and Progestin, Prednisone, Amiodarne, Cyclosporine, Anabolic Steroids, Protease Inhibitors and Diuretics

Conclusion: There is no significant difference between the Subject and Control Group with respect to HDL readings during Competition Phase at 5% (0.05) level of significance.

H_{A2}: There is a significant difference between the Subject and Control Group with respect to LDL readings during Competition Phase.

H_{A3}: There is a significant difference between the Subject and Control Group with respect to HDL readings during Off-Season Phase.